The Ultimate Teachers' Handbook

Related titles

Teacher's Survival Guide 2nd Edition – Angela Thody, Derek Bowden and Barbara Gray

Guerilla Guide to Teaching – Sue Cowley

How to Survive your First Year in Teaching – Sue Cowley

Primary Teacher's Handbook – Lyn Overall and Margaret Sangster

Secondary Teacher's Handbook – Lyn Overall and Margaret Sangster

The Ultimate Teachers' Handbook

What they never told you at teacher training college

Hazel Bennett

continuum
LONDON • NEW YORK

Continuum International Publishing Group

The Tower Building   15 East 26th Street
11 York Road   New York
London SE1 7NX   NY 10010

www.continuumbooks.com

British Library Cataloguing-in-Publication Data
A catalogue record for this book is available from the British Library.

ISBN: 0 8264 8500 6 (paperback)

Library of Congress Cataloging-in-Publication Data
A catalog record for this book is available from the Library of Congress.

Typeset by RefineCatch Limited, Bungay, Suffolk
Printed and bound in Great Britain by
MPG Books Ltd, Bodmin, Cornwall

Contents

To Graham, Russell and Alicia.
To the many thousands of pupils who have given me so much
pleasure and satisfaction.

Acknowledgements

I should like to thank these teachers and others for their helpful contributions to *The Ultimate Teachers' Handbook*.

Russell Bennett
Thomas Bleakley
Sue Brown
Debby Cohen
Carole Edwards
Fiona Eldridge
Catherine Gunn
Nicholas Gunn
Gene Henderson
John Hickman
Karen Kent
Joe Labuschagne
Emma Laikin
Kendal Maouchi
Samantha Nye
Catherine Paynter
Nancy Slack
Frances Smith
Renee Stanton
Penny Stevens
Cecilia Stevenson
Heather Toyn
Jacques du Plessis
Terry Ward

With special thanks to the writer Kate Nivison for her expert advice.

Foreword

Teaching is an interesting, stimulating and rewarding job. Though not highly paid in the lower echelons, it is still higher than nursing, and in some cases, architects and junior doctors. If you reach the top and become a headteacher, you can earn up to £80,000 in some inner-city schools, though you will earn every penny of it if you do.

It is a job which is full of challenges, and is exciting and inspiring for those with creative, inventive minds. For those who succeed, there's the reward of knowing you have guided pupils towards the ladder of success and most people remember with affection and gratitude a teacher who inspired them or guided them towards a satisfying career. Of course the holidays are an added bonus.

So why are some areas of the country constantly short of teachers? Why is it that there are often masses of vacancies which stay unfilled, in spite of the fact that the nation's universities send out more and more teachers every year? Why do so many teachers who enter the profession filled with enthusiasm and the urge to succeed fall by the wayside within the first few years, their expensive and hard-won qualifications wasted? Teaching has its pitfalls. Teachers spend a vast number of hours on tasks other then actual classroom contact, and this tends to wear them out and distracts them from the real job of enthusing the nation's pupils.

Preparing lesson plans in ever more copious and unnecessary detail and keeping progressively more detailed notes is tiring and time consuming. Reading new government documents and being disheartened by the regular changes which are imposed as soon as you have become accustomed to the last one is irritating. When examination results are announced politicians shout that the rise in grades represents a fall in standards, in spite of the Examining Boards' protests that they have observed a definite rise.

Coping with a pupil population who are increasingly aware

of their rights, and not always assuming the same need to consider their responsibilities, can at times be soul destroying, especially when you've spent valuable time trying to make lessons as appealing as possible.

We all know that competent teachers who can inspire their pupils to want to learn and ultimately become contributing adults are vital to the wellbeing of the nation. Of course our pupils deserve happy, stable schools where they can thrive and succeed. And who isn't aware that schools cannot deliver the best unless they are fully staffed and supported by management, parents and government?

Becoming an enthusiastic teacher who can rise above the difficulties and inspire pupils to succeed is a mammoth task but the rewards of job satisfaction and pleasure are just as great. The objective of this handbook is to offer teachers guidance in identifying the difficulties and to point out ways to rise above them, and hopefully encourage them to stay in the profession.

Part One

The induction year

(the bits you're not prepared for)

1 Starting off on the right foot

First day jitters. This is the information which they might have forgotten to give you at university.

After all your hard work at college, this can be a very exciting time. Don't be surprised if you feel your stomach quivering on the first day, because most newly qualified teachers (NQTs) do. For some teachers, the first time alone at the chalk-face is nerve-wracking. Schools can be a hot-house of pressure which one must learn to deal with in order to survive. Some teachers have a terrible time in their first year, leave the profession and never teach again. Fortunately, many who suffer all sorts of initial difficulties, rise above them, emerge with confidence and proceed to have satisfying and successful careers.

The most testing part is coping with a much longer working day than you were used to at college, and then going home to more school-related work. Even today, when NQTs have shorter contact hours than in the past, one has to cope with classes all day for the first time, which are stressful and tiring, leaving you less able to manage the extra hours.

If you work with a lot of experienced teachers, it can be unnerving as you watch them cope with ease. I have known young NQTs to put on an air of confidence or to pretend to know more than they did. This is unwise because the facade falls apart eventually and then teachers are less sympathetic. Always ask for help or information if you need it. No one can blame you for being willing to learn. Don't be afraid to admit to your colleagues that you're nervous. They were once nervous NQTs and they will sympathize and be all the more supportive.

The workload

In the weeks that follow, the list of daily tasks increases until you'll find yourself inundated. Your success in passing the induction year is co-measurate with your ability to handle the large workload. It is important to prioritize. When you feel you can't get everything done, write down every task that needs doing and number them in order of importance. Start working through the list and as soon as your head begins to ache, stop working. If you can't manage it all, leave the last tasks.

As long as you've put the planning in on time and prepared the lessons, you can probably postpone a few jobs. It is never worth persevering when you are tired because you make mistakes and become so tired and stressed that your performance level drops.

Teaching is very dehydrating so it's sensible to go to the staff-room for a cup of tea every playtime when you're not on play-ground duty. It's never a waste of time because the break and the drink help you to unwind if you've had a difficult session, and it's an opportunity to build relationships with your colleagues. Don't try to be an island. You need their support.

NQTs are frequently enthusiastic about taking on extra respon-sibilities, but do resist the temptation to start an after-school club in the first year as it takes about a year to establish a routine of planning, preparing and delivering lessons and marking efficiently. No one will think you lazy if you postpone the extra-curricular activities until your second year.

Dos and don'ts

The ship only sails smoothly if all the crew pull their weight and lean in the same direction. Regular staff absences lead to increased burdens on some crew members, a slowing down of progress and a few ructions along the way.

The first rule is: don't create waves. Teachers who have been in a school for many years don't want the place reorganized in line with the latest thinking on education. I knew an NQT who spent her first six months suggesting ways in which experienced teachers could improve their performance, and then couldn't understand why no one bothered to speak to her. Another failed his first year of teaching and had it extended, mostly because he inadvertently antagonized his mentor with his strong views. If you have ideas for reforming and improving the school, save them for your second year.

When the going gets rough, it's tempting to take some time off, especially as this is so easy in the days when you can sign yourself off for a week without a doctor's certificate. Try not to do it more than two or three times during the year. Teachers accept a certain amount of this from NQTs but their patience runs out eventually. It will be noticed if you malinger on days when it's your turn to take assembly, or your lessons are due to be monitored. Everybody assumes these are the reasons for your absence and it does your credibility more harm than turning up and underperforming.

Seize every opportunity to escape to the Newly Qualified Teachers' Inset during class time. It may become the best break you have in the week. When the older teachers in the staffroom enviously tell you how lucky you are because they didn't have any of that in their youth, smile sympathetically and say nothing.

The cast and crew

Know your cast and crew and, above all, their roles and how to interact with them. It is vital to keep them on your side. These include:

- the head;
- the school governors;
- teachers;
- the auxiliary staff – welfare assistants, secretaries;
- schoolkeeper, cleaners, kitchen staff.

The head
Being a headteacher is arguably the most difficult role in teaching. Most people involved, i.e. the teachers, the pupils, the parents, the governors and the inspectors all tend to suggest shooting the head for all that isn't going well. Those most eager to blame the head are the least likely to give him/her credit for all that does go well. Headteachers' responsibilities increase annually and the number who suffer nervous breakdowns or retire early with stress is on the

increase. With a double helping of pressure and power, it's not surprising that they tend to be rather an autocratic bunch.

Some say they're willing to be democratic and allow the staff to have a free vote in decision making, but usually they only do so on issues where they don't have strong preferences. I have even known heads to allow a vote but, when they didn't win, they ignored the vote and did what they wanted to do anyway.

A few tips

- In the first month, the head will regularly wander past your room and peer through the window in your door to see how you're faring. Find a large poster to cover the window before you start.
- The head will ask how you're managing. Smile confidently and say, 'Fine, thank you'. If s/he thinks you're having difficulty, s/he won't give you a minute's peace.
- If the head asks you to go on courses during your own time, refuse apologetically saying you need the time for planning and preparation.
- If the head chases you up about some job you've left undone, smile apologetically, and say, 'Thank you for reminding me. I have it as my first priority to attend to after today's marking, tomorrow's preparation and my appointment with Jimmy's mother'.
- Some heads are inclined to resent teachers who appear to question their judgement. Never ask, 'Why have we got to do . . . ?' Instead ask, 'Can you please explain the thinking behind . . . '
- It's not worth crossing swords with the head in your first year because you could not possibly win.

The school governors

The system of school management is quite unlike any other institution. Each school has a committee of governors, which includes the head; representatives of the teachers, non-teaching staff and parents; some local business persons; representatives of the Local Education Authority and the church or synagogue, if it's a denominational school. The number depends on the size of the school. In other words, people who are inexperienced and know nothing about running a school, can vote against the head, as can junior members of staff, secretaries or dinner ladies if they are governors.

The parents, teachers and non-teaching staff are proposed as candidates, frequently by themselves, and seconded by one other, and then elected by their peers and pals. Many parents are not interested and in some schools only a tiny percentage bother to vote. One of my friends proposed himself as a parent governor, was seconded by his wife and elected unopposed.

Understandably, this system frequently astonishes teachers from abroad who are amazed that people who have little knowledge of education can have power over the head.

The governors' tasks include interviewing and selecting staff, overseeing the budget, granting permission for pupils to be permanently excluded, hearing appeals of pupils who have been suspended, rubber-stamping promotion of staff and payments to staff on the upper pay spine, but usually much of this is delegated to the head.

Governors are a much maligned group of people and, like the rest of us, they vary enormously. Some governors, who are retired or are full-time housewives/husbands, are like gold dust to their school when they spend a day per week in school, helping in classrooms, going on school trips, running the school library and organizing fundraising events. Others rarely darken the door of the place during the school day, don't know the staff and do very little for the establishment.

Headteachers sometimes have ambivalent attitudes to them. If the governors are not well-educated, professional people, they resent having to obtain their approval for permission to permanently exclude a child, make a variety of changes and apply to them for their pay rise. If they are well-educated, professional people of some social standing, sometimes heads resent being scrutinized by articulate, confident people who can stand up to them and question their decisions, instead of automatically rubber-stamping them as the former type may do.

Some teachers complain that the governors don't come into school often enough and then don't bother to make them welcome when they do, so it could be worth cultivating their goodwill by making them feel welcome. The more they feel appreciated the harder they'll work for the school.

If they're parents, you'll probably have their child in your class one day, and they'll support you better if you've already developed a friendly working relationship with them. If you apply for a post of responsibility, you may have to face them across the interview table. Remember too that if you intend to stay in the school for years, they also make the final decision, based on the headteacher's advice, about whether you receive later increments on the upper pay spine.

It is rare for governors to give individual teachers any problems, but a few don't understand the parameters of their roles. Individual governors don't have any real power over individual teachers. If you think a governor is imposing on you unreasonably, a tactful answer is, 'I'm not sure if I can do that. I'll have to ask the head's permission,' and follow it through.

If you think they're not making the correct decisions, the only real solution is for you to stand for election and be a teacher governor yourself.

Being a school governor is a thankless task. They aren't paid for their trouble, and are sometimes resented. Not surprisingly, it's usually very easy to become a governor, because most schools have difficulty in finding enough people.

If you do join a governing body, it's important to go on a training course to obtain a clear view of the extent of your responsibilities and the limitations of your power.

It is also important to make it a priority to attend every monthly meeting. I have known heads who suffered great frustration caused by governors who regularly failed to turn up because they had something better to do. Likewise, it's vital to carry out any task accepted, quickly and efficiently.

Teachers

Your mentor
To help you to stay on top of it all, you'll have a mentor, an experienced member of staff, who's been allocated the task of showing you how to cut your teeth without drawing blood. It is wise to form a positive working relationship with him/her, because s/he can encourage and guide you through the difficulties, or undermine you until you give up.

Some mentors mother NQTs through their first year. Others do little for them. If you do have a mentor with whom you cannot get on, approach the senior member of staff with whom you have the best relationship and explain your problems in a purely factual manner, being careful not to create acrimony. In extreme cases the head will change the mentor, but only if you have a good case.

Other teachers
You should also try to form a friendly relationship with other experienced teachers in the group, as they can support and encourage you through the fray.

- Always be civil to the ambitious teachers on the staff. One of them might be your next head.
- Be equally kind to the unambitious teachers. They will keep you sane when end of term madness invades the school.
- If you're an ambitious teacher, be respectful to everyone, because next year when you have a post of responsibility they will be much less cooperative if you have spent your induction year irritating them.
- If you're not an ambitious teacher, it's fine to stay that way. It increases your chances of survival.

The auxilliary staff

School secretaries
They will know every error you make on the school registers and requisition forms. Irritate them, and all your misdemeanours will be relayed to the head. If you have a happy relationship with him/her, s/he may type your letters to parents and make phone calls for you. Annoy him/her and you will have to do it all yourself.

School caretakers
They should be handled with care. The speed with which they fix anything broken in your classroom or fetch heavy bits of equipment, is often in direct proportion to the kindness you have previously shown them. When s/he moans at you about what a raw deal s/he always gets, look sympathetic and say **nothing**. A small number are bossy and awkward. Never let them push you about. Be polite but firm, with answers like, 'I'll have to check that with the head,' and follow it up. Report intimidating

behaviour to the head at once, with expressions like, 'He appeared to be threatening . . . ' Happily the last piece of advice is rarely needed.

Cleaners

Always speak kindly to whoever cleans your classroom because you may need to ask him/her to keep an eye out for small pieces of apparatus that go missing during the day. A box of chocolates at Christmas works wonders.

Classroom assistants

They are a luxury for which we never dared to hope in the 1970s and 1980s. They are paid a derisory salary for light behind-the-scenes jobs, like saving the class teacher from having a nervous breakdown. If treated kindly, they will put up your classroom displays, do your photocopying, nip out of class to fetch the resources you've forgotten, sharpen the pencils and all the irritating chores. It is wise to give them a lot of encouragement and gratitude, in case they start looking for a better paid job. Never ask them to mind the class for you. It's taking unfair advantage of them and they will support you much better if you treat them fairly.

Some older teachers resent unqualified people like classroom assistants working in the classroom. It's best not to go down that road. A competent professional should not feel threatened by non-professional people, and in any case the pupils need all the help they can get. Remember the aim is to survive and be a successful teacher, not maintain the purity of the profession.

The kitchen staff

If the school meals are edible, and some aren't, it's worth being pleasant to the kitchen staff and throwing in the occasional compliment to the cook. You get a higher level of service, and larger portions of food if you're in favour with them.

Also, when you keep a child in at lunchtime to finish his/her work and you inadvertently release him/her after they stop serving, they are less likely to complain to the head when you ask them to stop clearing up and provide the child with lunch.

2 The parents

Always start with the premise that parents and teachers both want the child to be happy and succeed, and so they should be on the same side and support each other. Usually parents and teachers maintain a friendly relationship, which benefits the child and promotes a positive attitude to school work.

Some newly qualified teachers (NQTs) are wary of parents. This is understandable because in a small minority of cases, they can be a never-ending source of grief. Alternately they can halve your difficulties and be a constant source of support. So it is important to treat them with the same care as the pupils. Always remember that you're dealing with their most precious possession and so allow for a modicum of rose-coloured judgement on their part.

Like their children, they vary enormously. There is no need ever to feel threatened by parents who are themselves teachers. I have often found them quite sympathetic, because they understand the difficulties with which you have to cope. Many are a tremendous bonus. If they come on school trips they know exactly what is expected of them and do not wander off to the café or the pub, unlike some who think they've been invited because you wanted to treat them to a day out.

Try to avoid confrontations with parents because they often lead to more problems than they solve. As with pupils, never back them into a corner, otherwise they will come out fighting. Try to give them an escape route and keep their goodwill because you have to teach their child until the end of the year, or longer, in secondary school. You may also have to teach their siblings in later years so it's worth keeping the path smooth.

Building a positive relationship

Think ahead. When you receive your class list(s) for the following year start looking out for the new parents and approach them with a comment like, 'I'm having your Freddie in one of my classes, next year (smile and look pleased about it, especially if you aren't). Do pop in and see me occasionally to see how he's getting on'. You'll be amazed how far a little bit of goodwill goes. Of course if you work in a school where the parents don't have jobs outside the home and want to stay for an hour on a regular basis, ignore this point.

Some of these tips might help.

- It's important to start on the right foot. On first meeting a parent always start warm and friendly. Let them see you as a kindly person, interested in their child.
- Get to know their names as soon as you can. If they are step-parents or have a different name from the pupil, try to get it right. They appreciate that.
- Some families have complicated lives. The 'father' is occasionally a live-in partner. Try to be sensitive, and stay in touch with the real father as well.
- Many pupils live with carers. I always try especially hard to build a harmonious relationship with them, because they have the children who need most support.
- It's best to be approachable, not aloof. Always smile, speak or nod if you run into them.
- Make sure the child realizes that you see his/her parents as your friends.

Preventing difficulties

- Make sure you tell parents what you expect from pupils – homework in on time, politeness, punctuality, etc. Explain or remind them of the school policy on any issue where there's disagreement. Use expressions like, 'As I'm sure you are aware, the school's policy on this is . . .'
- If they say your demands are unreasonable, explain the reason for them and the possible consequences of their child's action.
- Be a good listener.
- Try to avoid confrontations. Humour often works.

- Never let a parent know if you dislike their child.
- On first meeting parents, if they look tense, or their child has a track record of misbehaviour, greet them with a smile and say, 'Ah yes, he's a loveable little rascal, isn't he' (primary). Another useful expression is, 'I quite like your son because he is . . . ' and mention a few of his good points (secondary).
- If they're becoming argumentative, turn the conversation round by asking questions like, 'What do you think are his/her weaknesses/strengths?' It's a non-aggressive way of guiding them to acknowledge their child's less endearing qualities.
- Record details of all meetings in case it has to be referred to later. If the parent is known to be difficult, make sure they see you scribbling notes and your writing is illegible upside down.

Dealing with difficulties

- When you have a worse than average difficulty with a child, it's wise to call in the support of parents before the problem grows. If you leave it a long time until, say, parents' night, they will give you the answer, 'If s/he's been giving you that much difficulty you should have told me much sooner so that I could sort it out'.
- Explain your problem in a calm, factual manner. Try to keep negative adjectives out of it, in the first instance at least.
- If a child settles down and improves after you've spoken to the parents, look out for them and tell them how pleased you are. Thank them for their support. They need reassurance too and a simple word of thanks builds a bridge for the future. Remember, you might get one of their other children in a future year.
- Never verbally attack parents unless they attack you first. If you have a problem, start positively by saying something like, 'I feel I really need your help here. Your son is a lovely, polite boy and he tries hard with his work. I like having him in my French class but can you please remind him to bring in his homework book each Friday because I haven't seen it for a month'.
- If they won't listen to you or let you get a word in, wait until they have finished, smile and say politely, never sarcastically, 'I have listened to you patiently for ten minutes. Will you listen

to me now for the same time please without interrupting?' If they still won't listen, finish the meeting immediately.

Parents' consultation evenings

Most schools have one, two or three per year. You have between five and 15 minutes to establish a positive relationship, inform parents of their child's progress and answer their queries. NQTs, and even some experienced teachers, and parents have also told me they're nervous beforehand.

Preparing for the evening
- Forewarned is forearmed! In a primary school, have a chat to the previous class teacher and find out in advance if any parents are likely to be difficult and in what way. In a secondary school, ask the class's previous year's form teacher.
- Look again at the Home and School policy, to remind yourself of its details. Have one in your drawer. It is handy to have it available to back up your argument if the parents are unsupportive.
- It is difficult to keep all the information in your head so make notes on any issues you have to raise.
- Clear all the untidy heaps off your desk and replace them with all your record books so that you have information at hand if needed.
- Stop the last lesson of the afternoon ¼ hour early to tidy up the classroom. Give each child a job and it should be done quickly.
- If you're intending to show pupils' work, then ask each child to have their books out in individual piles with a name label, on chairs outside the classroom if possible.
- Try to have the books marked up to the previous day's date at the latest.
- If the meetings begin soon after the pupils leave, always make sure you have at least a short break for a cup of tea and a snack. An afternoon of teaching is thirsty work.
- You may feel more confident if you bring a change of clothes to school for the event. A discreet wash and change can make you feel fresher and more confident.

The interviews

It is best to adopt a pleasant but professional manner. Be friendly but not familiar. Keep a discreet distance between you. The following might help.

- If it's your first time and you're anxious, try to get a support teacher to sit in the interviews with you, for the difficult parents at least.
- If you have a timetable of interviews, try to stick to it as closely as you can. Keep a watch or clock on the table if you can't see a wall clock. If a parent comes late, don't over-run to compensate. It annoys the next parents on the list. If a parent comes very late, try to avoid letting them push in. Offer them another date. If you do over run, apologize to the parent whom you have kept waiting.
- When parents come in, stand up to welcome them with a smile and offer your hand. Likewise when they go, thank them for coming and for any help or support they've offered.
- If they're known to be aggressive, take up a formal position behind your desk. Otherwise sit facing them in the body of the classroom, on a chair the same height as theirs.
- Never have more than one set of parents in the room at a time, unless it's a large room and you can comfortably talk to parents without others overhearing.
- Make notes of any issues to be followed up as you go along, because it's difficult to remember it all after you have spoken to a long list of parents.

The vast majority of parents approach consultation evenings in a spirit of goodwill, but a small minority view it as an opportunity to air their grievances or to try to catch the teacher out. I have known a small number of parents to admit that that's their purpose. Parents' questions can vary from the intellectual to the trivial.

Frequently asked questions and suggested answers

Q How do you assess my child's capabilities?

A Give a run down of the tests which you use, e.g. reading and spelling tests, NFER tests, QCA or SATs, GCSE tests and school's own examinations.

Q How do you monitor progress?

A Look at test (SATs, QCA, etc.) results and compare them to the previous year/term. Or

A I look at the beginning of the exercise book and the end and compare the two.

Q Will my child be held back by less able pupils?

A No, we always provide more stimulating work for the brighter pupils. Give details.

Q What's your discipline like?

A We try to maintain a peaceful atmosphere with a system of rewards and incentives. Explain the details.

Q So far this term, a coat, two caps, three pairs of gloves and a peashooter have been stolen from my child. What are you going to do about it?

A He has lost his homework book, two library books, three school pens and a few CDs. We'd like them back. Could you deal with this for us, please? Or

A Explain lost property procedure. Emphasize that if the item is named, you do your best to return it to the correct person. If not, there is little you can do.

Q Before my child came to this school, s/he was happy, lively and full of enthusiasm for learning. Since coming here s/he has lost interest and says that it's not worth getting out of bed.

A We were hoping you could tell us why s/he is so demotivated. Or

A Could it be hormones? Or

A Has s/he made friends here?

Q My child says s/he hates you because you're constantly blaming him/her for everything that goes wrong in the class. Why do you do it?

A Because s/he normally is the one to blame. Or

A I do blame others when they misbehave, but they usually accept a rebuke with a better grace.

Q Our child is lovely with everyone except you. Don't you realize s/he hates your style and that's why s/he won't work for you?

A I can please all pupils some of the time and some pupils all of the time, but not all of them all the time. Or

A Pupils have to get used to lots of different teaching styles just as teachers have to cope with a wide variety of abilities and willingness to work in pupils. Or

A It's a preparation for life, getting on with a wide variety of people. If none of these work, as a last resort,

A Oh dear, I hope you're not going to have to take him/her to a shrink.

Q Our son doesn't mean to harm other pupils, he's just having a little game when he's fighting.

A When he gets into a fight outside school, try using that excuse with the police and let me know their reply.

In most cases, teachers and parents form a friendly, mutually supportive, relationship but, unfortunately, it sometimes breaks down. The following are suggestions on how to handle a minority of problems.

Coping with aggressive parents
- Whatever happens, try to stay calm and in control.
- Occasionally you can diffuse a situation with humour before it becomes nasty.
- Pass the buck if you're young and inexperienced. Let the head of year or head of department cope with the hassle.
- If a difficult situation arises unexpectedly on parents' night, don't let it develop into a heated argument. It is better to make the suggestion, 'We need to discuss this more fully, can you come back and discuss it when we have more time,' and make an appointment there and then. When they return for the next interview, make sure you have a senior member of staff present and have notes ready, as it can be difficult to think on your feet.
- It is often helpful to have a pupil's books ready in case you want to prove that the work is or is not up to standard or shows a lack of care.

- If the parent is behaving in an intimidating manner or looking down their nose at you contemptuously, stare them out with an unblinking grin, as if you haven't noticed. It is difficult for them to keep it up if it is having no effect.
- For parents who raise their voices, start wagging their fingers, or banging their fists, say calmly but firmly, 'I'm sorry Mrs Smith. I'm not prepared to discuss this while you are behaving in such an uncivil manner. Either you calm down and we discuss the matter like adults or we will have to have this interview at a later date'. If they refuse to calm down or move, stand up and look at the door and say, 'If you would like to return and discuss this when you are calmer, that's fine'. If they still refuse to calm down or leave, walk out.
- In extreme cases, write up your notes and pass them to your head or head of department.
- Never show any fear or dismay. If they turn up unexpectedly with daggers flying out of their eyes stay calm and say, 'Oh Mr Bloggs, I'm so glad to see you. I was going to send for you'. Then start describing the child's latest misdemeanours.
- Make it clear you're not intimidated by threats. Counter, 'I'm going to the head,' with, 'That's fine. Off you go then,' and stand up, forcing them to either go or back down. If a complaint comes back to you from the head, make sure you point out that the complaint to higher authority was being used as a threat against you. Have all your facts ready.
- If you can, try to speak to the head before the parents do, because it also makes it easier for the head to deal with it if s/he knows the facts in advance.

Violent parents
It is still rare for parents to physically assault teachers, but teachers' unions and associations confirm that it is on the increase.

- If parents are known to be violent towards their children, be careful to speak positively about their children to them. It's heart-breaking to discover that pupils have had a harsh corporal punishment after you've informed the parents of their misbehaviour.
- If you have an appointment with a parent who is prone to

violence, have a senior colleague, preferably the head, with you and try to keep a broad table between you.

- If a violent parent turns up unexpectedly, say, 'Can you wait a moment please,' and fetch the head or head of year. Never allow yourself to be alone with him/her.
- If a parent hits you, ask your union for advice and support fast. Take legal action. Your union or professional association should provide you with legal cover. This is why it's mad not to be in a union or professional association.

How to cope with the whingers
In the past, some elements of the media, and even some members of the government, had negative attitudes to teachers and encouraged parents to question everything in their children's schools. Although this situation has improved in the last decade, there's still a tiny minority of parents who rarely express any appreciation and are permanently looking for an opportunity to complain.

It can be difficult because sometimes we have to face the fact that they may be right. You have to know your pupils and parents well to be able to differentiate between the parents with genuine complaints, which must be taken seriously and acted upon positively, and those parents who complain regularly as a matter of course and to whom you must stand up to politely but firmly.

It is wise to have answers ready.

- If they complain that the work you're giving is too difficult, try, 'I am trying to stretch the pupils. They need to be stimulated to reach their full potential'.
- If they say the homework is too much, a reasonable compromise might be, 'Let him/her spend 30/60 minutes on it, and I shall accept that even if it's incomplete'.
- It they complain that the work is too easy, try, 'Tracie never mentioned it, but if you're sure, I could set her some extra homework'. Or, 'I don't mind trying her on harder work, but of course if she can't manage it, I shall have to put her back to what she's doing at the moment'.

It may be an opportunity to show his/her work to the parents and tell them what s/he needs to achieve before you can give him/her something more difficult. Or, if examinations are looming, it may be appropriate to say that you're revising to consolidate everything you've already done.

If they complain there is not enough homework, it may be worth mentioning that the pupils have worked hard all day and need a break to do other things to allow them to come back to school refreshed. You will need to justify this, so refer to any examination results, QCA results or class assessments to reassure the parent that their child is not being held back. Similarly, show them their child's books to reassure them they are achieving an acceptable level. If you're not actually giving homework, it is best to face the fact they're perhaps right and start setting it.

If they say their child is bored in your lessons, get out any attractive text books or apparatus you use to show them. Refer to any school trips or videos, which you have used to make the lessons more interesting. Describe how lessons are organized, because often parents do not realize how much trouble teachers take to make lessons enjoyable and stimulating. If you think they're more interested in complaining than the quality of education, I would suggest one of the following: 'Perhaps you could explain to Ali that you only get out of your work what you put in. If he put in more effort instead of spending the lesson trying to worry the gerbil, he would get more satisfaction from it'. Or, 'I think it's rather fashionable to be bored at the moment. Most of the pupils in the class are quite interested in their work. I'm afraid it's down to Ali to put in the effort'.

If that fails try, 'What do you do when he is bored at home?' If they become really stroppy about it, as a last resort you could frown and say, 'If people are bored, it's their own fault, and they can do something about it. I'm never bored and I'm not sympathetic towards anyone who is'.

How to answer complaints about victimization – the 'you're always picking on my child' syndrome
Remember, occasionally they may be right because sometimes pupils irritate you so much, you find yourself inadvertently nagging them more often than the others.

Describe the child's behaviour quietly, in a purely factual manner. Explain how you've dealt with it and why. Involve the parents with comments like, 'If you can suggest a more effective way of dealing with it, I am willing to listen to you'. Show that you respect their views and they can become supportive rather than confrontational. Try to give the impression that you like their child in spite of his/her misbehaviour. It's sometimes easier to keep the parents on your side if you start positively. I often say, 'S/he's a good pupil in many ways but it is difficult to keep the pupils on task while s/he is calling across the room and disturbing the pupils who want to get on with their work, etc'.

If they complain that you're victimizing their child by keeping him/her in at playtime to work, point out that you're worried s/he is slipping behind the others, because of time wasted in class. Again, describe how s/he avoids working and emphasize that you're anxious that s/he may slip down a set, have to go into a special needs group or end up with no GCSEs. Try to get across to them that your main worry is their child's progress and future success.

If the parents don't believe you or still insist that you're victimizing their child, then you can turn it round and say, 'That's fine, next time s/he spends the morning faffing about, doing no work, I'll ignore it, but don't come complaining to me that s/he has made no progress at the end of the year'.

When they complain that your punishment for their child's hitting another child was too severe, just say, 'That's fine, next time a child punches your Jimmy, I'll be more lenient'. Give them details of how their child has inflicted pain on other pupils and ask them how they would respond if the same violence was inflicted on their own child. It is amazing how some parents have a different set of rules for how a teacher should deal with that issue, depending on whether it's their own or other people's children who do the punching and kicking.

Parents are rightly quick to complain if their child is bullied. If there has been a complaint against the child, tell the parents about it but not the identity of the complainant. Parents are subject to peer group pressure as well as pupils and knowing that other parents resent their child's behaviour frequently makes them back down.

The 'I know my rights' brigade
I find these people insufferable in any circumstances. The more they shout about their own and their children's rights, the less

they care for anyone else's, and the less responsibly they and their children behave.

When they complain that by sending their child out of the class for misbehaviour, you're depriving him of the education which s/he has a right to have, point out that keeping her/him in the classroom would be depriving the other pupils of the education which they have a right to. Try, 'I am expecting the other pupils' parents to complain about your child's disruptive behaviour and I intend to treat them sympathetically'. You may even have already had complaints. If so, tell them, but never disclose which parents have complained. They will never trust you again if you do.

Generally, when they launch into a speech about their child's rights say, 'You've taught him/her his/her rights, but have you taught him/her to respect everyone else's rights? Have you taught him/her his/her responsibilities?'

When they assert that a child has no responsibilities, you can quite justifiably become teacherish and say something like, 'Of course they have. A child's responsibilities are to be kind to other children because they want other children to be kind to them. They have to respect other children's property because they don't want others stealing or breaking theirs. They have to obey the adult who is looking after them because no one can keep them safe otherwise. They have to tell the truth because no one wants or trusts a dishonest child, and they have to try hard with their school work to help them get on in life. If you get all that into pupils' heads by the age of 5, they'll give you no trouble and you'll be rewarded with the admiration and respect of other parents'. I've done it. Parents are so taken aback after listening to all that, they don't know what to say.

A very tiny minority, possibly because they suffered too much corporal punishment themselves as pupils, love to remind teachers and others that no one has any right to touch their child, and if anyone ever lays a finger on him/her, they'll sue for assault. If their child is fairly manageable, I would just smile and say, 'No problem,' and change the subject. If their child is prone to violent behaviour, look concerned and remind them that now he is over 10 their child can be taken to court and sued for assault. Remind them that there are in the UK today, children as young as 11 in secure accommodation for crimes of extreme violence.

Some of this might paint a dismal picture to a new teacher, but remember that these are a tiny minority. In many schools parents rarely present problems and are a constant source of help to teachers. Most parents are respectful, supportive, friendly and even grateful. Although you must try to have a friendly working relationship with parents, you must also make sure they treat you with respect. Never let them order you about. The rude, overbearing parents often back down or even give up when they realize you're not a pushover.

Don't feel too bad if you do occasionally cross swords with parents. I've never known a teacher who has ever achieved a peaceful relationship in every case.

3 And what are we here for? The pupils

Pupils can sniff out a weak teacher as s/he dawdles hesitantly through the doorway. If you stammer, avoid eye-contact, or speak in an over-ingratiating manner, you'll immediately become a target of derision. Always keep your head up, your shoulders back, smile confidently, look them in the eye and speak as if you're taking it for granted that everyone will cooperate. Try not to look apologetic.

Your success with each class will depend on your relationship with them. Make sure you start on the right foot. Try never to lose your cool in the first lesson with any class, as it makes it horribly difficult to regain the pupils' trust. When they have become accustomed to your funny ways, it won't matter too much if you lose it occasionally.

Teachers are usually nervous in their first week, so go to the loo just before you enter the classroom.

Building a positive working relationship

- In a secondary school, meet and greet the pupils at the door. This also ensures a punctual start to the lesson.
- In a secondary school where you have different classes, of up to 30 pupils, a day, try to direct a question to each child, each lesson. It's difficult, but it helps to build up a positive relationship.
- At lunchtime, or in the corridor, nod or speak to pupils, if appropriate. They appreciate being valued and aloofness leads to the breakdown of a relationship.
- Sarcasm is the lowest form of wit! If it works at all, it's temporary and is counter-productive in the long run.
- If there's someone in the class whom you particularly like, try to hide it in case the 'teacher's pet' syndrome arises.

- Similarly, if you dislike a child, hide it at all costs.
- With shy pupils, say a few encouraging words to them quietly as they leave at the end of the lesson.
- For future years, running after-school clubs helps to build up good relationships, but note that this is not a wise idea in the first year.

Motivating yourself and the pupils

The key to keeping pupils interested is being enthusiastic yourself. Pupils are quick to spot a lack of interest on the teacher's part. It's impossible to carry pupils along with you unless you can communicate that your lesson is worth having and is of value to them. However you feel, crack on that you're loving it. Use expressions like:

- 'This is what I enjoyed at school'.
- 'This is my favourite bit'.
- 'Last year's class loved this'. (They don't know this is your first year.)

Use lots of incentives like:

- 'If you can all finish this before the end of the session, we won't have any homework'. (Only use this one when you're not giving any homework anyway.)
- 'The table that's tidied up and ready first will go out to play first'.
- 'I know it's hard to concentrate on Friday afternoon, but if you can give me and hour of concentrated work, you can have the games out for the last half hour'. (Primary school.)

Primary pupils, and even some secondary pupils, love tangible rewards like stickers or certificates which you can run off the computer, ten minutes extra play for the whole class, if the head permits, even sweets but only if you're absolutely at the hair-tearing point. Never make the prize too attractive or expensive, because it raises the pupils' expectations.

Someone will probably accuse you of bribery and corruption in the case of the last two, but I would just smile and say, 'Nonsense! We all need a reward to work towards'. But I would never use sweets in front of an inspector.

Positive attitudes work best

It's so easy to point out mistakes and give negative instructions ('no, that's wrong'; 'don't do that') and so difficult to keep pupils interested after you've done it too many times. Often teachers are perplexed as to why pupils are so turned off, and are unaware that they themselves have actually disheartened them. Put yourself in the pupil's place and imagine how you would feel if the only comments you got were negative.

When a child gives a correct answer, say:

- 'Brilliant!'
- 'That's clever of you!'
- 'I can see you are good at this!'
- 'You've obviously got a very mathematical/scientific brain!' Any old lie will do.

When a child gives an incorrect answer, try to give answers like:

- 'Nearly right.'
- 'That's half right.'
- 'A sensible/intelligent guess!'
- 'Keep trying, you're almost there!'

When an answer is so far wrong you cannot say anything encouraging, say no gently and make a mental note to say something encouraging later in the lesson.

When it's difficult to engage a child in his/her work, start the lesson by asking an incredibly simple question and allowing him/her to answer. Then look delighted and say, 'Fabulous!' Repeat each time his/her attention wanders.

Organization – don't underestimate its importance!

Organization is vital. If you've forgotten some of your resources, you have given the pupils a delightful opportunity to play merry hell while you're distracted rectifying the situation. You also look as if you aren't sure what you're doing. Pupils are quick to deride a weak teacher and only respect and cooperate with teachers who look as if they're on the ball.

- Always make extra worksheets because someone is bound to mess it up, or a new child will join the class. But don't be too free with them otherwise the pupils think they should automatically have a new one each time they make a mistake.
- If worksheets are differentiated according to ability, have the ability group discreetly marked on the sheet. It's irritatingly simple to mix them up while you are simultaneously answering someone's question and sorting out misbehaviour.
- In your classroom choose the notice board closest to your desk and pin onto it: your timetable; the names of the pupils in each group, or class in a secondary school; the week's literacy and numeracy plans (primary) and other weekly plans (primary and secondary); and the sets of worksheets. It prevents them from being lost under atlases, dictionaries and the last set of sheets.
- Always keep spares of each type of exercise book ready for when pupils run out of space. If you don't they might seize the opportunity to mess about while you send out for one.
- If you work in a school where there's a high turnover of pupils and you're given new pupils without notice, keep plenty of spare books ready.
- Allocate each job to a pupil: tidying up shelves, returning science apparatus to its correct place, returning books to the library, etc. Remember if a job is not assigned to someone it won't be done.
- Always have a rota system for allocating jobs to pupils. They like the fairness of chores being shared evenly.
- If you use a lot of worksheets you can end up with millions of pieces of paper. Have a system for storing them, such as a folder for each child, keep the folders in alphabetical order and train the pupils to file their own work away.

4 The thorny issue of discipline

'Frequently called behaviour management'

This is a subject not adequately dealt with in some universities and colleges. Many teachers begin their career believing that they have an automatic right to each child's respect and cooperation, and in many schools it's a harsh lesson to learn that respect must be earned. Class control can make or break a teacher. A fair to middling teacher with good discipline can survive gracefully. An articulate and inventive teacher with brilliant ideas and poor discipline will have a hard time.

It takes a clever teacher to master the art of making sure the pupils want to do everything the teacher's way.

Starting off on the right foot

Your ability to control each class is largely determined by the quality of your relationship with them. Discipline-wise, the first lesson you have with each class is the most important, because here is where you lay down the foundation for your future working relationship. If you start off well the rest falls into place more easily. If you and the pupils rub each other up the wrong way, it can take a long time to mend the situation. Most of the following can apply to either primary or secondary classes.

- Start each lesson on time; set the tone that they have to be present and prepared at the start of each lesson. This is especially important in secondary schools where pupils are changing class and have every opportunity to be late.
- Speak respectfully to pupils. Some teachers are quick with a cutting or belittling remark, which may work in the short term but stores up trouble for the future.
- When you acquire a new class, learn their names quickly. If

you don't address pupils by their names when delivering an instruction or a rebuke, it's so easy for them to ignore you and pretend they thought you were talking to someone else.

- Use a quiet, firm and polite manner to lay down your parameters before you start.
- Some teachers spend the first half hour negotiating an agreed contract with the class, by establishing ground rules, of what teacher and pupil reasonably expect of each other, and pinning them up on the notice board. This works fine as long as the teacher sticks to his/her side of the agreement. For example, if the teacher agrees to mark the books each day/let the pupils out to play on time, and then does not keep it up, the contract falls apart easily.
- If you think you can't cope with being consistent with a two-way contract you may find it easier to just lay down the rules and describe the consequences of them being ignored.
- Make it clear what you want pupils to bring to each lesson.
- If you know in advance that a pupil is likely to be tricky, it's a good idea to ask a teacher who has worked with him/her what works best.
- Alternately, catch him/her out doing the **right** thing. When they're doing what you want, say, 'That's cool, Simena'. It is so much more effective than rebuking them for doing the wrong thing.
- Establish a clear and simple routine to your lessons. This isn't boring and humdrum; pupils like to know where they are and what's coming next.
- Always prepare much more work than they can handle. The devil soon finds work for idle pupils.

The 'don't' list

- Never actually lose your temper. I did it twice during my first term – once when I was told to 'go back to Ireland, you flippin' Irish git,' and once when I was kicked in the shins and told to 'fu★k off'. If you lose control of yourself, you cannot possibly control them. You can, of course, have a controlled loss of temper, i.e. just pretend to have lost it. It can work if you do it on rare occasions only.

- Never back a child into a corner from which they cannot escape, otherwise they'll come out fighting. Try to always give them an opportunity to get out of a tight corner and conform.
- Never trap yourself into an upward spiral of punishment, from which neither of you can escape. It leads to disaster. If punishment does not work after two or three attempts, try a different strategy.
- When pupils threaten to bring their parents to the school to sort you out on their behalf, don't look dismayed. Lift your diary and say, 'That's great, I was hoping to meet them, I'm free this afternoon, bring them in'. I have never known a parent to turn up after that.
- Try not to shout at pupils for misbehaviour. (Well not any more than you have to.) Noisy teachers have noisy classes. It has more effect the less often you do it.
- Never shout to attract attention from a noisy class.
- Never imagine that you know it all. I have been teaching for over 30 years and am still learning new strategies. If you make mistakes be prepared to learn from them.

The 'do' list

- Try to stick to the school behaviour policy as rigidly as you can.
- Be consistent. Pupils are quick to spot an inconsistency.
- Always give a clear explanation if there's a change of procedure. No one likes to be confused.
- Listen to pupils. They love it, especially the worst behaved. Often they don't have enough opportunity for conversation at home.
- Have a system for attracting everyone's attention. Some infant teachers rattle a tambourine. I always say, 'Hands up those who are listening,' and follow it up by adding, 'Good, Jimmy, you can go out at playtime,' to whoever's hand goes up first. Another effective trick is to release first at the end of the session the group who were giving their attention first. In a secondary school saying, 'Quiet please, thank you. Quiet please, thank you. Third time, quiet please,' often works.
- When a child is messing about when they should be working,

start with, 'Can you manage? Would you like some help?' Not, 'Stop talking/stop messing about/don't be so lazy'.

- When you get comments like, 'I'm not doing this, I don't want to,' smile sweetly and say, 'No problem, you can do it at lunchtime'. Or, 'That's fine. You can take it home and do it. I'll speak to your parents and tell them. They won't mind'. Whichever works best with the individual child. This often works, especially after you've carried it out a time or two.

- Remember pupils who don't respond to threats and sanctions often respond to praise. Use lots of it on disruptive pupils when you can.

- Give positive instructions: 'Please work quietly,' not, 'Stop talking'. 'Write slowly and carefully to keep it neat.' Not, 'Stop rushing through it and making a scruffy mess'.

- Before imposing a sanction, give pupils a clear chance to conform. For example, 'Your behaviour is not acceptable, you have got from now until lunchtime to get yourself back on track or your lunch break will be spent in here working with me'.

- Always try to impose sanctions, the same day if at all possible. They lose their effectiveness if they drag into the next day.

- In one school where I worked, there was a system whereby pupils could earn a release from a sanction if they changed their behaviour and conformed. It sounds like letting them get away with it. But as long as their conforming to proper standards was substantial, it worked.

- Seating arrangements can alter pupils' behaviour. Seating boys beside girls sometimes calms either one of them down, or hardworking pupils beside those not so desperate to learn.

- Keep notes about any serious incidents in case there's any problem with parents later.

- Keep the praise flowing, but not so much that you devalue it.

Handling classes with disruptive pupils

If you find yourself facing a class with lots of problems, including poor behaviour often caused by poor teaching, poor parental support and a high turnover of teachers, you will need lots of positive strategies. Keep incentive schemes running. They work much better than constant threats and punishments. These are a few strategies which have worked well for myself and many of my colleagues in the past.

All discipline strategies work with some pupils, and all pupils respond to some strategies. If something doesn't work, don't despair, because no one has ever got everything right first time. Just change the strategy.

The positive approach

Team points

I have known teachers to make disorderly classes work quietly by dividing their class up into four teams, each with a snazzy name, and putting a chart with each name on the wall and giving each team a point/sticker when they have worked quietly for a session, tidied up first or all brought in their homework on time. The team with the most stickers at the end of the week gets a small prize. Always keep the prizes small or you end up broke. You can often find a pound shop or market stall where they sell packets of marbles, jars of bubbles, tennis balls and small novelties at four for a pound.

This works well in a primary school. In a secondary school, letting pupils off a homework task is an attractive incentive, but of course make it revision homework so they can't be left with a gap in their knowledge.

Merit boards or star charts

These are for individual good work, and are a good incentive. All the pupils' names are down the side of the chart and pupils are given stars or stickers opposite their name for good work or behaviour. You can give a prize, like a chocolate orange, at the end of the half-term. Make sure the stickers are for effort as well as quality of work, so that the slowest child in the class has as good a chance of winning as the most able. Someone on the staff might disapprove because it's competitive. Smile calmly and say, 'But life is competitive. It will be good for them to learn to cope with it while they're young'.

Golden time

This is an effective strategy. Some schools use it as a basis for the whole-school behaviour policy. The pupils are allotted 30 minutes at the end of Friday afternoon to do some enjoyable activity of their choice. If they misbehave during the week, they can have golden time taken from them in five-minute slots. When the time arrives, they have to sit for the time withdrawn from them and watch everyone else enjoy themselves. However, so that the pupils who have lost all their golden time by lunchtime on Monday have some incentive, they can earn it back again, in five-minute slots, if they mend their ways.

Star of the day

At the end of the school day, the pupils are invited to nominate pupils who have shown most care and consideration for others/ positive attitude/most effort with their work. The one with the most votes is named on the star of the day chart and the next day gets a reward, for example, a cushion for when they all sit on the carpet for that day.

A special mention box

A shoebox, covered in brightly coloured paper with a slot in the top and the words 'Special Mention Box' on a prominent label, is placed in an available position in the room. Pupils write down details of any kindness they've had from another child and put it in the box. They're all read out at the end of the week before golden time. It works because pupils love self-esteem and the child who writes the special mention often feels as good as the one who receives it.

Names in the jar

A colleague of mine used to keep a jam jar with a lid, and every time pupils showed an improvement in attitude, effort, progress or care for others, their name was written down and put in the jar. At the end of the week the one pulled out at random got a reward, like being let off a homework task.

Marbles in the jar

This is a whole-class strategy. If your class is habitually noisy, tell them there'll be a marble in the jar for each 15-minute working session, lining up and going to assembly and sitting quietly through-out, where everyone, emphasize everyone, remains quiet. When the jar is full, everyone gets ten minutes extra playtime. You need the approval of the head for this one.

Sweets in the balance
An inventive colleague of mine brought a packet of sweets into school and took a weight balance out of the maths cupboard. He put a mass of 100 gms into one side of the balance and every time a child showed improvement/effort, etc. he ostentatiously put a sweet into the other. When the balance eventually tipped, the child who had earned the last sweet got all of the sweets in the balance. That worked beautifully, especially when the pupils realized the balance was about to tip.

Fabulous fun trip at the end of term
For the horrendously difficult classes. You can only do this with the head's support. Two of my colleagues told their ultra-challenging classes there would be a strictly fun, non-educational trip at the end of term for those who deserved it. A black dot chart was pinned to the notice board alongside the brightly coloured poster advertising the venue of the trip, and a nasty little black dot placed beside the name of each pupil each time they did not follow instructions promptly. Those who had an unreasonable number of offending dots were left behind in school with work to do in another class, as the rest of the class lined up for a day of fun. The improvement in attitude and behaviour was a delight to watch.

Each one of these works well with classes if they're carried out consistently. You can experiment and see what works best with each class. Obviously, if the pupils are well behaved and interested in their work, you don't need all these schemes.

Confrontations and avoiding them
Some teachers say, with some justification, that if you get into a confrontation you've already lost. Some say you've only entirely lost if the pupil in the end doesn't bend to your wishes. In either case you have certainly had your image tarnished, because the pupil has challenged your authority and probably caused amusement among his/her peers, gaining him/herself some kudos and embarrassment for you. Try to avoid confrontations, at all costs, because they generate acrimony which frequently takes a long time to subside.

If you think one is about to arise, try to diffuse it with humour in the first instance. If that fails go up to him/her and whisper, quietly giving two choices and describing the consequences in each case. That should give him/her an escape route.

If that fails, say, 'I can't waste time on this now, we have too much work to get through, we'll have to discuss it at lunchtime/break time/end of the school day,' and keep a discreet distance between yourself and the pupil. If s/he continues to behave in a loutish or disruptive manner, say calmly, 'You are clearly not in a frame of mind to take part in this lesson, take five minutes out until you have calmed down and return when you are feeling better'. It's best if during the five minutes s/he is physically in the classroom. Warn the others not to interfere with the pupil, while s/he calms down. If the pupil calms down and joins in the lesson, never refer to the episode again. We all need our sins to be forgotten.

If a child storms out of the classroom in a temper, your reaction should depend on whether the school premises are secure and the age of the pupil. There is no need to follow unless s/he is an infant or lower junior child in a building where the gate is unlocked during the day. They usually come back if you ignore their exit. If s/he does not return by the end of the session, you will have to check up on his/her whereabouts, to ensure his/her safety.

At all costs avoid a screaming match, disruptive pupils love it and whatever the outcome, your image will suffer much more than theirs as a result.

If you know that someone is about to throw a tantrum, keep a few metres between him/her and yourself, smile and say, 'You can throw a tantrum if you like, give us all a laugh!' It often pre-empts it, but if it doesn't, make sure you do laugh. Don't, under any circumstances, let any emotion other than amusement show. They won't be so eager to try it again if all they receive is ridicule.

Above all, never give in to a child who has thrown a tantrum. It's like throwing buns to crocodiles: they are bound to repeat the process for more.

Coping with the 'I'm going to wreck the class' mob

In many schools, pupils will conform if treated reasonably, but unfortunately there's sometimes a tiny minority who are determined to destroy the lesson, however much time you've put into making it interesting, enjoyable and fun.

Try these strategies outlined below.

- If you've been warned that a pupil in your class is a right pain, make a point of saying something positive, like one of the comments mentioned earlier (see p. 26), to him/her in the first lesson. If they know you regard them as hell-raisers, they'll make a concerted effort to live up to your expectation.
- If a child tries to wind you up by passing wind in your lesson, ignore it and at the end, discreetly keep him (it is normally a him) back and tell him you'll be asking his parents to teach him a little anal control if there's a recurrence. Never comment on the matter with other pupils around.
- Be strict about each detail with every class for the first term and by then you should have cracked it. In some schools you can only survive by keeping it up all year.
- If a child is disruptive, send for a parent early in the school year, before a problem grows too great. Approach the parent in a friendly manner, emphasizing that you're concerned about the child's progress. Ask if there's anything in school which might be upsetting him/her and throw in a comment about something s/he is good at. Then you can say that s/he has wrecked a variety of classes since the beginning of term and you're concerned that s/he will not make progress, or other parents might complain.
- In a secondary school, make sure you and they know the sanctions and the chain of command – form teacher, head of year and senior teacher, for dealing with misbehaviour.
- Depriving a child of an activity which they enjoy – swimming, football – often works. In a secondary school you must clear this with the PE teacher first. Ignore the pupil's protests that s/he is entitled to those activities. Brush aside the retort, 'I have a right to . . . ' with, 'It's not a right, it's a privilege and you'll only get it if you deserve it'.
- When you hear the protest, 'That's not fair,' counter it with, 'It's perfectly fair because it's for your own good. You'll realize that in 30 years' time'.
- Only make realistic threats because once you've done so you must carry it out. If you say you're keeping a pupil in at lunchtime, you undermine yourself if you then relent.

Building bridges
- If, after admonishment/sanction, the pupil conforms, lavish loads of praise and appreciation on him/her.
- Never bear a grudge. When the day is over, put it behind you and start the next day as if the previous day's unpleasantness never took place. Pupils (and adults) appreciate that.

Rights, again
The days of 'when in doubt, clout,' are long gone and today's pupils have more rights than the teachers, and they know it. It is usually the least respectful and most aggressive pupils who love to say, 'My mum says no one has any right to hit me. If any teacher ever lays a finger on me, my parents will take them to court and sue for assault'.

The answer is, 'That's right. No one has any right to hit you and you have no right to hit anyone else'.

If the pupil is already over 10, tell him/her that **s/he** can be taken to court for acts of violence and that in the UK there have been pupils, as young as 11, detained in secure accommodation for acts of violence.

I used this line many years ago with a severely violent child, and was easily able to resist the urge to be sympathetic several years later, when I was informed that he had spent some time in one of Her Majesty's centres with all expenses paid.

If you can teach your pupils the glorious lesson that everyone else has exactly the same rights as themselves, you've done them a tremendous favour.

End of term syndrome
At the end of each term, try not to let up the pressure of work any sooner than you can help. Keep the pupils working as far into the last week as you can. Once you've dropped the work habit, you'll not be able to restart it until the following term and the devil soon provides entertainment for pupils who are not occupied with something either enjoyable or worthwhile.

5 Paperwork, planning and other time-consuming chores

Paperwork

One huge bugbear of any type of teaching today is the copious amounts of paperwork. In the Inset days before the pupils arrive in school, you'll be accosted by various senior staff treating you to a generous helping of written information.

When the head offers you the school handbook, look pleased and say, 'That looks interesting'. If the document is under 1 cm thick (and this is not a joke), take it home and read it. These ones are usually well-written, tend to be succinct and contain most of the information you need to be going on with. If it's much thicker – some are up to 8 cm thick – put it on the shelf and refer to it when you need information. Never ask the head for information, until after you've consulted it first. If what you need is in the handbook, it irritates the head to know you've not read it.

In most schools there is a notice board in the staffroom and teachers usually have their own pigeon-hole or in-tray. Through either one of these you will constantly receive flyers about courses, new books on the market, places for class visits, offers of people to come in to school to give educational workshops, updates on school policies, LEA policies, DfES policy documents, notification of oncoming school events and minutes of staff meetings. This is by no means a finite list.

You could not possibly respond to it all and still have the time and energy to teach properly. The clever bit is knowing what must be taken on board or dealt with at once, what must be kept safe for later and what must be filed in the wastepaper bin (wpb) or scrap paper tray. I have a system whereby the urgent stuff goes on the notice board by my desk so that I can't lose or forget it.

If you've a working area at home, it's worth photocopying the really important stuff, like the school holidays, to pin on your home notice board as well. I keep a ring binder marked 'staff information' for all the school data and anything which might be useful later. It is sensible to have another for school policies. Anything which I'm sure I won't need goes in the scrap paper tray or the wpb.

Being organized is vital. It saves you the irritation of wasting your precious time, three months later, searching for a flyer about a school workshop which looked useful. Also other staff become annoyed with you if you lose some piece of school information which they've spent time typing up for your convenience.

Planning

In pre-national curriculum days, teachers used to draw up a loose plan for the term and work their way through it at the unpressurized pace that they considered suited the pupils' rates of learning and their own sanity.

In those lax, easy-going days, timetables were loosely administered in a primary school and teachers did their lesson planning and preparation as the week progressed. Heads rarely asked for forecasts and record keeping was minimal. Compared with today's stringent practices, little was written down and when asked for a record of work done, the response, 'The work in the pupils' books is the only record you need,' sufficed. Frequently teachers decided what to do the previous day and sometimes while on the journey to work that day. (Them were the days!)

The curriculum was nothing like as regular or rigorous as it is today, but teachers suffered much less stress and the atmosphere in the classroom was frequently less tense, and despite what some elements of the media would have you believe, the pupils did actually learn and enjoy it. In those golden days of teacher autonomy, the enormous freedom afforded to teachers gave an opportunity for their individual flair to shine out and inspire their pupils.

The requirements of the national curriculum and the accompanying forecast of medium-term objectives, assessments, targets and evaluations have put several hours of labour per week onto the teachers' workload. Overseas teachers who are unaccustomed to it complain that having to write plans in such minute detail leaves them with less energy to present the lessons with vigour and enthusiasm. However, it must be acknowledged that better plans, on the whole, lead to more interesting and better organized lessons.

Remember your plans are your servants, not your masters. If during the week, you think of a better idea, don't be afraid to change the details.

A few tips to save time

- If you are new to the year group, or if it's your first year and the previous year's plans have not been handed to you, always ask for a copy of them. It's foolish to reinvent the wheel.
- If you work in a year group where there are parallel classes, split the planning into two or three, photocopy your lesson plans and worksheets and swap. It is time-economic for one person to run off the worksheets for the two or three classes for their area of planning because it's as easy to copy 30 as 90. It also lessens the queue at the photocopier.
- If the head tells you that all lessons have to be planned in unison, don't argue. Just sit in the same room and each of you do your own half/third and then all of you swap your work and everyone sign each piece.
- The weekly plans usually have to be handed in on a certain day each week. If you make it a priority to have them in on time, the head is more likely to have faith that you are doing everything properly. If the plans are often late s/he is more likely to keep checking up on you.
- Try to discreetly find out whether the senior staff actually read them or not. A friend of mine asked the deputy head if he read the plans and got the reply, 'Read them? It takes me an hour to file them!' I know another case of an English teacher who wrote a list of nursery rhymes under the heading of 'Poetry' for his A-level class to test if the head read them and the plans came back signed without comment. If they are not read, obviously you need not be quite so diligent in the detail and presentation.
- In primary school for weekly literacy and numeracy plans, the most efficient way is on the computer. Some things are the same each week so if you superimpose each week's lesson on top of the previous, or a similar, week's plan you only need

to amend the words. I managed to cut my weekly literacy planning time in half doing this. And ICT is definitely not my forte!

- Keep a copy of every medium-term and weekly plan and worksheet, all neatly organized in ring binders with file dividers for each topic. At the end of your first year ask the head if you can stay in the same year group, so that you can consolidate everything you've learnt this year. Another reason is, of course, so that you can re-use all your plans and at least save you hours of planning and preparation next year.
- Try to save time by using commercially produced worksheets where possible.
- Heads sometimes tell the staff that all planning and preparation is the property of the school and must not be removed from it. This is technically accurate but normally honoured in the breach. Most teachers with an eye to the future keep a copy of everything at home in the filing cabinet or at least stored on a floppy disk. You may be able to use it all in your next school.

Marking

Time consuming and tedious as it can be, this is important and worthwhile because it's an integral part of the teaching process and unlike some paperwork tasks, it does actually benefit the pupils. Most well-organized schools have a whole-school policy for marking to make it easier for pupils to understand if their work is marked by several teachers per week. If there's no whole-school policy, you will have to organize your own, and in either case, make sure the pupils understand it.

Make marking constructive for the pupils

This can apply to either primary or secondary classes. Put on your wall a chart with an example of each mark and what it means. For example:

//		new paragraph
_____ (sp)		spelling error
( )		leave this bit out

✔ (in the margin)	an interesting or clever expression/point to make
✘ (in the margin)	This bit is wrong
_____ (gr)	grammar error
～～～～～	this bit doesn't make sense
N.R.	– not relevant (secondary or upper primary)
N.A.	– not applicable (secondary or upper primary)

When you give the work back, give the pupils a few minutes to look through it to see their mistakes and invite them to ask you about anything they don't understand. You can make your marking helpful and encouraging with the following points.

- Use an erasable Papermate. They are good for erasing your own comments when you want to change something in view of something you read later in the essay.
- Try not to mess the pupil's work up with great slashes of colour. A short deletion line is as effective as a long one and not nearly so disconcerting.
- Experts on dyslexia say you should never use red, or any bright glaring colour, to mark the work of pupils with learning difficulties. This is understandable, since it's so disheartening if their work is returned covered with red marks. I always mark these pupils' books with a black pen or lead pencil with a much darker shade than the pupil's writing.
- If a piece of writing is completely riddled with errors, try to find an opportunity to take the pupil aside and ask him/her to read it to you. Write at least a few of the sentences out underneath for the child to see the correct version. It's clearer for him/her and not so depressing as masses of marks across the work.
- Spelling corrections arise out of writing activities. Pupils with learning difficulties can only manage one or two at a time. Dyslexic pupils can manage one or two per week. The rest up to a few per piece. Use your own judgement depending on the age group and what the child can manage.
- You don't need to correct every error in every book. Gauge it to the individual child. If there are only a few errors per page, I mark them all. In the average book, mark several of the most obvious ones on each page.

- At the end of a writing lesson, give pupils time to confer with each other in pairs and look at each other's work to find their own, and each other's mistakes.
- Write positive comments to encourage pupils to correct their weaknesses. For example, 'I like your ideas and choice of vocabulary, but try to concentrate on keeping it neat as well,' not, 'This handwriting is dreadful,' even though it might be.

Class marking

Take a piece of work done by a child and blow it up from A5 to A3. You can make this an acceptable practice by saying to the child first, 'You don't mind if I use yours do you?' Tell the class you've chosen Mandy's piece because you're so delighted with it and start by pointing out a few positive things about it, like neat handwriting or interesting vocabulary.

Invite the pupils to mark it one sentence at a time. Providing that this is done in a positive manner with constructive remarks, it should not cause embarrassment to the child. I have done it on a regular basis and found pupils were pleased when their work was chosen and it also helped pupils to learn to correct their own work.

Use stickers and stampers with words like 'excellent', 'terrific' and 'super work'. They save you time and even lower-secondary pupils love them. If you teach modern languages, you can buy stickers with 'tres bien' and 'sehr gut'.

A few pointers to take the strain off you

If some work can be marked in class with pupils marking their own or another's book, always do so. Five minutes of class time can save you an hour of your own time. I always pre-empt pupils from cheating by saying the following, 'You could easily bump your score up by rubbing out any wrong answers, putting in the correct ones and pretending you got it right on your own. Is there anyone here who would be silly enough to do that? I shall not say a cross word to anyone who has every answer wrong, but I shall be disgusted with anyone I find cheating'. It doesn't seem worth the bother to cheat after that.

- While the pupils are working at something which they cannot mark as a class in unison, walk around the room and pick their books up one at a time and mark what they've done. This not only saves you time, but enables you to point out mistakes to pupils as they go along.

- If you are severely under pressure, during silent reading lessons you can discreetly mark books while you have a confident reader beside you reading. It's not good practice so it's better not to make a habit of it: only as a last resort if you fear the job is getting on top of you.
- Always collect books open at the right page, so that you don't waste precious time leafing through each book looking for the work.
- Try to mark at the most time-economic point in the day. Some teachers who commute save time by marking on the bus or train. If you walk or drive to work it's often easier to mark in school where there are fewer distractions. If you have young children of your own, it's sometimes easier to take the books home and leave school earlier to spend quality time with your own kids, and mark when they're in bed.

Everyday chores

Paperwork is not the only tedious chore. There are plenty of time-consuming tasks around the classroom. I like to cultivate the good-will of the pupils who hate going out in the cold in the winter. They are usually willing to spend playtimes sharpening the pencils, tidying the book shelves, filing pupils' completed worksheets in their folders, cleaning whiteboards, taking work off the wall and cleaning out the hamster's cage.

If you do a lot of sports activities in secondary, it's worthwhile selecting a reliable pupil to do the communication work of notifying team members about events, even if details are posted on information boards. This is a two-way benefit because responsibility teaches pupils reliability and adds to their self-esteem. If a pupil becomes a regular supporter throughout the term, an occasional gift of a book token or similar is appropriate.

6 Taking assembly

Taking assembly in front of the whole school, or at least a substantial part of it, is a task that most teachers have to face eventually in their first year. In some schools the list is put on the staffroom notice board with everyone's name written beside a date. In primary schools, considerate heads do not normally force NQTs to face the ordeal in the first half-term, but you're less likely to avoid it in the second half. In secondary schools, where there's a larger number of teachers to share the rota, you may escape a little longer.

If the rota is blank for everyone to put their name after their chosen date, make sure you nip in fast and put your name at a date convenient to you. Otherwise you'll be left with the space that no one wants, like the first week of term when you're bogged down with so many other new things to get used to, or the end of term when you're too tired to think about it, the pupils are restless and you have too many other things to do, like report writing and marking examination papers.

Each school has its own format for timing, organization and content. You will either have to take an assembly solo, or organize the class to do something entertaining, or perhaps both. I find doing it solo easier because it takes about a tenth of the effort needed to organize and rehearse the pupils, but many teachers are so nervous about standing up in front of the whole school and staff, they always organize the class to provide the entertainment instead.

Even some very experienced, competent teachers who are so self-assured in other circumstances have told me they need to run to the loo a couple of times in the hour before assembly. I even had a colleague once who was so anxious she offered to do my playground duties for several weeks in return for my doing her assembly.

In your first year in any school, in the weeks leading up to your turn, it's wise to make a few mental notes about how your colleagues do it. Timing is important. You can discreetly time how long each teacher speaks or the class activity lasts. Heads don't like teachers to over-run or cut an assembly short. Note if the school has costumes or props, how to get them and the type of items presented. Some schools keep a record of each assembly and it is wise to look through before you plan because it would be embarrassing if you duplicated one done recently.

School policy on assemblies

You will also need to look at the school policy. Each LEA has an agreed syllabus for RE and collective worship in maintained schools. It must reflect the fact that the religious traditions of the UK are mainly Christian, while taking account of the teaching and practices of other principal religions. Maintained schools must provide daily collective worship, usually through assembly, but in some schools this is honoured in the breach unless there's an inspector present. Voluntary-aided and foundation schools with a religious character will determine their own policy.

The good news is that you don't have to worry about the school policy sticking strictly to the letter of the law because it's the head's responsibility. If s/he does not object to the content of your assemblies then you have no problem.

Some schools have a high percentage of ethnic minority pupils for whom mainly Christian-based assemblies would be inappropriate. These schools can apply to the local Standing Advisory Council on Religious Education (SACRE) for a determination to have this requirement lifted. It is best to read the school policy and then see how it is put into effect by watching your colleagues.

Don't be a shirker!

It is unwise to try to opt out of taking assembly on religious grounds. If you take a secular assembly, it is unlikely that anyone will object. If you try to opt out completely you could be viewed as lazy. If you find it nerve-wracking in your first year, ask your mentor for support, or another teacher with whom you have a harmonious working relationship, to do a joint one with you. Sometimes two classes join up and do two joint assemblies instead of one each.

Generally, if you admit you're anxious about something your colleagues will support you. If you try to shirk a responsibility their sympathy can dwindle.

Planning an interesting assembly

My best advice is to read *Assemblies Made Easy* by Kidwell (2004). It is a humourous book with lots of brilliant ideas, slickly written with pithy dialogue.

Some schools have a theme which changes every half-term. I find these rather restrictive, but if your school has this policy there's very little you can do about it.

If you have a free hand, but are short of ideas, here's a few to try.

Religious festivals

Look at the current calendar prepared by the Commission for Racial Equality (CRE) or SHAP. They tell you the dates and times of most religious festivals and celebrations. Most schools have one or the other but, if not, you can get one from them direct.

CRE's main office is at: St Dunstan's House, 201–211 Borough High Street, London SE1 1GZ. Tel: 020 7939 0000, or fax: 020 7939 0001. Their Publications Department is at: 0870 240 3697, or email info@cre.gov.uk. Details of their local offices are on their website www.CRE@tso.co.uk.

You can contact SHAP at: Shap Working Party, PO Box 38580, London SW1P 3XF. Tel: 020 7898 1494, or fax: 020 7898 1493, or their website: www.shap.org. The SHAP website also gives details of other websites which allow you to download their calendar of religious festivals. I found a good one at: www.bradford.gov.uk/ art/religious-festival/pdf/ReligiousFest.2005.pdf. The print is very small as it's compressed onto A4, but you can use the school photocopier to enlarge it.

Alternatively, if you just want information about one particular festival, you can usually put the title into www.google.com and get plenty of information.

Saints' days

These can be fun. Even if you're not a religious person, lots of saints have an interesting story behind them and pupils love to act, mime

and tell stories in assembly. You can get information about each
saint on the Internet – just type the name into www.google.com.
Infopaedia CDs usually have some information on each saint, and
don't forget the good old-fashioned *Children's Britannica* and the
Penguin *Dictionary of Saints* by Attwater and John (1982).

Present a resumé of something you're studying in class
For example, if you're studying the Victorian period, a short
Victorian drama with a news vendor shouting 'read all about it!',
followed by a documentary of a few important Victorian events
mimed or dramatized by the pupils. It reinforces all your class work
and the pupils love doing it: think of it as a revision activity.

An account of a school trip
Pupils love to present a resumé of outings. If you've taken slides or
digital camera photos, reproduce them on a screen. Pupils are always
pleased to tell about an event in which they're pictured.

Look around your neighbourhood or within a few miles radius
Is there an interesting building with a history? Has someone well
known lived or worked there? Is there a park, museum or cathedral
with an interesting story? Cities, especially London, are crammed
full of interesting places. The closer to home, the more interesting
the story will be.

Aesop's Fables
For Key Stage 1, these are a simple way to teach a lesson for life.
Children love to tell, act out or mime a story and tell everyone the
lesson to be learnt.

Use topical sporting events
These work well for Key Stages 2, 3 and 4 – the Olympic Games,
the latest marathon, the World Cup or Wimbledon. These are of
premium interest to the pupils, especially secondary, and you can
always find some moral or life skill to be held up as an example of
good practice. Is there a performer who has demonstrated great
courage and perseverance? Is team spirit an important issue? Has
one of the team overcome some horrendous difficulty to succeed?

'Modern day' saints

There are plenty of people whose character, courage and devotion to others is exemplary – Mother Theresa, Gladys Aylward, Florence Nightingale, Mary Seacole, Nelson Mandela, Martin Luther King, Mahatma Gandhi, Maximilian Kolbe or Christopher Reeve.

Anniversary events, jubilees, independence days, Thanksgiving, national days – for example, Australia Day

For these, get out maps and show children where they are. Look on the Internet – I am a fan of www.google.com to find information. Tell the pupils how they came to be governed by a foreign power, how they achieved their independence and who were the people who brought it about. You can put together a presentation of the events.

'On this day, seventy years ago . . . '

In your local library there's probably a book telling about events which took place in the past on every date in the calendar, for example, *On this day in History* by Mayo and Jenkins (1989). You are bound to find something interesting.

Who's your hero?

Jane Austen, Freddie Mercury, Walt Disney, Henry Ford, Thomas Edison, Charles Dickens, Mozart, David Beckham, Elvis, J.K. Rowling, Ellen MacArthur. Whoever you chose, each one is a fine example of something – talent, courage, perseverance, generosity, hard work, devotion to others or a determined pursuit for justice.

Key Stage 1: birthday assemblies

These are held once per month with a mock cake and candles and are a fun event. Teachers and/or classes take it in turn to provide entertainment with a birthday theme. If you visit your local library, you will find lots of lovely story books with a birthday theme.

In the best one I've seen, a teacher put on an apron and prepared a cake with odd ingredients – vinegar, onions, mushy peas, etc. and sent it off with another teacher to be 'baked' while everyone sang 'happy birthday' and a had a few pieces of light entertainment. The cake was then brought 'back from the oven' with pink icing and smarties for the birthday pupils to share.

Solo assemblies – a few hints

Preparation and rehearsal

- Whatever the topic, plan your opening line or questions to interact with the pupils. I always start with a few simple questions. For example, if it were St Andrew's day, 'What date is it today?' 'What's special about today?' 'Put your hand up if you or your parents are Scottish?' This grabs their attention and distracts them from the conversation they were trying to have with their neighbours.
- Practise it aloud and time it to make sure it fits the slot allowed.
- Learn the script: never read.
- Prepare a few visuals to keep the attention of pupils, particularly infants. Overhead projector acetate sheets are handy. Making them is not too time consuming. I just trace the outlines and ask for a pupil to volunteer to stay in at playtime to colour them in.
- If your ICT skills are up to it, you can place your visuals on a PowerPoint display. They look impressive, keep the pupils interested and impress the head.
- If you are using a cassette tape or CD player, make sure you know where the power points are and use a reliable machine that you've used before. If it's a tape, make sure it is all set ready at the right place.
- Plan a final line which finishes the story off well. Write it down if necessary.

On the day

- Make sure that you and your class are the first ones into the hall.
- Keep a glass of water handy.
- For background music, as they come in, play something pleasant but soothing, not loud or lively because it makes it harder to settle them down.
- If you feel at any time you're losing their attention, ask a few more questions to get it back.
- Fix your eye on a child and make eye contact and then slowly move your eyes around so pupils feel you're addressing them personally. If you're nervous and fear you may lose your place,

it helps to write about ten key words on a scrap of paper and glance down at it discreetly about once or twice a minute.

- A bit of play acting helps to keep their attention. Put on different voices for different characters, mime a few of the actions while narrating and exaggerate your facial expressions.
- Don't forget the music on the way out.

Class assemblies – why they are worth the extra work

These are time consuming to prepare but well worth the bother. Pupils love people listening to them, and it gives an opportunity to shine to pupils who don't have much chance to shine in class. I always try to give the less able pupils as prominent a part as they can handle. Pupils who are attention-seeking in class often thrive in front of an audience.

Pupils can be nervous beforehand but overcoming it is just part of the process of growing up. Performing in front of an audience is an invaluable part of their education because it builds up their confidence and self-esteem. In schools where there are regular class assemblies the practice often enhances the quality of end of year productions and Christmas concerts.

Planning

- There must be an element of fun, so the pupils will want to perform and so that the audience will enjoy listening. Try to throw in a few jokes.
- The assembly should have an objective: a lesson to be learnt.
- The lesson doesn't have to be something with a high moral tone. For example, in the third week of April the objective may be to awaken the pupils' interest in the life and work of William Shakespeare.
- If you have an objective of the last type, you could add the moral that if you have a talent, you should use it to enrich your own and everyone else's life; or if you want to do something exciting with your life, work for it, reach for dreams, aim for the sky. There's always something.

Practising

- Pay special attention to clear speech which can be heard at the back of the hall. Teach pupils to lower the pitch of their voice to raise the volume and to speak more slowly. For the first practice, I sit at the back of the hall, and say, 'I can't hear you,' whether I can or not.
- It helps to share the workload. If you want them to sing a song, ask the music teacher. If you want them to do a dance, ask the PE teacher. Specialist teachers are usually helpful about letting the pupils practise during PE and music lessons, or at least playing the music onto tape for you to use to practise or showing you how to organize a dance.
- If you're using a long poem or a story, try to split it up into as many parts as you can, even if you have 20 narrators with a few lines each. It means everyone gets a turn and no one has too many lines to learn.
- As with solo assemblies, try to make sure everyone memorizes their part. Reading it never has the same effect.

On the day

- Pupils in Key Stage 2 often want to dress up for assembly. This could lead to hours of extra unnecessary work. If there's a school costume cupboard, fine. Otherwise tell the pupils that costumes don't matter but if they want one, they must provide it themselves.
- Emphasize that it's the quality of performance which really counts.
- As with solo assemblies, don't forget the music for entry and going out.
- At the end of the performance publicly thank any of the staff who assisted you.

When it's over

- Mentally evaluate. I always judge the quality by how well the audience sits still and listens. Make a note of anything which might be helpful for the future.
- After you've stopped sighing with relief, lavish lots of praise, house points and stars, etc. on the class afterwards.
- If someone has made a mess of something, it's best just to

laugh and tell the child it doesn't matter. My stock line is, 'Don't worry Freddie, I've made much bigger bloomers than that'.

- Keep a record of every assembly you do. I have a file with all my notes, overhead projector acetates and notes retrieved from the Internet. This is not another useless piece of paper-work. You can use them in your next school or in the same school if you wait for about four or five years.
- If another member of staff has had a large input, a box of chocolates or a bottle of wine is appropriate to show your appreciation.

7 Organizing day trips

School trips. Why bother?

There has been much controversy surrounding school trips in recent years. Each year in schools in the UK hundreds of thousands of pupils go on school day trips and return to their parents safely and happily, having benefited from the experience. Unfortunately, a small number have resulted in minor accidents, and in a few extreme cases, tragedy, generating understandable grief and anger on the part of sadly bereaved parents.

Some teachers who have successfully undertaken trips for years are now anxious at the prospect of facing parents if the worst happens, or the shame and strain of court proceedings if an accident takes place and charges are pressed.

Litigation is becoming a popular trend of our society and with numerous companies touting for business with slogans about blame and claim, teachers feel they're in vulnerable positions. Some unions have advised their members against undertaking school trips for fear of being sued if an accident happens. This may be an understandable reaction, but I fear it is an over-reaction.

Every day in life someone is killed in a car accident, but that does not stop anyone from going on a car journey. If we all take the view that we must not undertake trips, then we end up with the situation where no one does anything extra to enhance pupils' experiences, and education becomes a bland, less exciting and less stimulating experience.

I have always enjoyed school trips and thought them well worth the extra work. The advantages are manifold.

- They're great fun and a break from the humdrum routine of the classroom.
- They provide pupils with hands-on experience which

reinforces your lessons and transforms theory into reality. For example, a trip to Butser Ancient Celtic Farm brings the Celtic period to life. A trip to a Shakespeare play or film inspires the pupils who were not inspired by the black print on the page.

- In the follow-up lessons in school in the days which follow, the quality of pupils' work always shoots up.
- It's an effective bonding experience. Your pupils' allegiance towards you increases when you give them an exciting day out.
- Pupils are so pleased that you've taken them out they usually behave better on trips.
- School trips awaken pupils' curiosity about the world and increases their urge to find out more.
- They can be used as rewards for good behaviour and exclusion for bad behaviour.

A few minor drawbacks

While I am such a keen believer in the value of school trips, I have to report with regret that there is a downside.

- Contrary to the opinions of some outside the profession, they are much more tiring than a normal day's work.
- They involve an extra load of tedious paperwork – insurance rules, letters to parents and collecting their permission slips and collecting money.
- The dangers are bound to increase when you take pupils through the gate and on to the road, and you are responsible for their safety.

Planning the trip

You're unlikely to have to take overall responsibility for planning a trip in your first year, but you'll probably have to assist with one. For the future, when you're planning a trip always visit the venue's website in advance. In the week or two before the trip you can often use it to plan an ICT lesson or devise one in conjunction with the ICT teacher.

You also need to visit the actual site, even if it's quite far away. If it's very far away, your school should help you with travel in the form of a train fare or petrol allowance, although you may have to visit it in your own time.

Use this as a checklist to find out what you need.

1   The opening and closing times.
2   The entrance cost including all the adults. Some places allow teachers in free if you explain that you're coming with a view to bringing your class there and some allow all accompanying adults in free on the day of the trip. Some add the condition that free entrance is in return for keeping the pupils quiet and well behaved.
3   The location of all the toilets.
4   All of the facilities and educational activities which are available to schools, their costs and how much notice must be given to book them.
5   Is there a room for the pupils to eat their packed lunch? If not, try to find somewhere suitable.
6   The gift shop. Look at the prices and estimate how much money you think is sensible for the pupils to bring. If it's overpriced, it's best to exclude it from the trip. You also need to find out if there are rules about how many pupils they allow in at once.
7   Plan work for the pupils to do, or things for them to find out while there if appropriate. Some museums and cathedrals provide worksheets. Check if they're pitched at the right level for your class. You may need to prepare your own, or amend their sheets.
8   The location's safety policy. You may need to sign an agreement to abide by it.
9   Decide the mode of transport. If booking a coach it must be done well in advance.

The letter to parents
Even at secondary level pupils can only be taken on trips with parents' written permission. You must write a letter to parents giving the following information.

1   The date and location.
2   One sentence explaining the objective, for example, 'to consolidate their topic on the Romans in Britain'.

3   The mode of transport.
4   The cost. In state schools you must say that it's voluntary and no child will be excluded for non-payment.
5   The times of leaving and returning to school.
6   Ask the parents to make sure their pupils bring any of the following which are necessary:
    - packed lunch – no glass or nuts as other pupils may be allergic;
    - waterproof jacket or mackintosh;
    - carrier bag to sit on if you'll be eating out of doors;
    - pocket money allowed – it is best to suggest a modest amount;
    - something to amuse themselves on the journey if it's a long one and confirming that each pupil must be responsible for its safety;
    - medication, for example asthma inhalers, pills in a named container to be given to the first-aider;
    - sensible footwear – trainers, wellingtons, change of socks.

Ask the parents to sign the permission slip and state whether their son/daughter may return home alone after the trip if it's after the normal home time. Always remind them that pupils cannot be taken on a trip without the written permission and set a deadline which is about a fortnight in advance of when you really need it.

In a state school, if parents are unable to pay, the school must accept the cost, but if the permission slips are not signed and returned then, sadly, the pupils must be excluded. I have known this to happen and it causes pupils understandable grief, as well as giving the teacher the extra chore of setting work which the pupils can do without support, and finding another teacher to have the pupils in his/her class for the day. That is why it's best to leave yourself plenty of extra time to chase up the parents who consistently forget about it.

Paperwork
There are, of course, a few common sense precautions.

1   Read your school policy on school trips and as long as you make sure you stick to the letter of it, especially the safety precautions, you cannot be blamed if anything goes wrong.

2   Take more adult helpers than the school policy demands –
    classroom assistants, part-time staff, parents or governors. The
    cost does not matter: safety does.

3   Check the insurance. If you are taking parents or people who
    are not members of staff, they may have to sign something to
    include them on the school's insurance for the day. Check
    with your mentor/head/environmental studies coordinator.

4   There is probably a risk assessment questionnaire to fill in.
    It's best to do it well in advance so that you have time to
    organize anything extra which the head asks of you.

Adult helpers

- Choose your parent and governor helpers carefully. I find the
  best parent-helpers are the ex-teachers because they know
  how much responsibility they must take on and don't imagine
  that the day out is a relaxing treat for them.

- Remember parents need to be checked out by the police for a
  disclosure of any criminal record just as teachers and other
  school staff. Some schools keep a register of willing parents
  who have been checked out by the police for the purpose.

- Always give parents who are not being paid for their day's
  work an easy group of well-behaved pupils.

- If bringing a parent who has never been on a school trip
  before, always explain any safety procedures and emphasize
  that the pupils cannot be left unattended at all. I know a parent
  who nipped off to a café for a cup of tea and a sandwich during
  a trip.

- Give each adult helper a pack containing the timetable and
  organization for the day, the class groups and their leaders, each
  leader's mobile phone number, information about the venue
  and a copy of the work the pupils are to do during the day.

The pupils

Always make it clear that:

- Only those who can behave perfectly will be going. This
  is an absolutely reasonable request. Remember that pupils,

especially teenagers, like to push the boundaries out. If you want excellent behaviour, demand perfection.

- Anyone who lets the side down will be excluded from any further trips and **make sure you carry it out**. Failure to do so undermines your discipline for the future and antagonizes the pupils who have made the effort and had their day spoilt by the misbehaviour of others.
- Serious misbehaviour will result in their being immediately escorted back to school. This is another reason for having extra adults. Unfortunately you can only say this if it's practical for you to carry it out. You look weak if you make the threat and then don't follow it through.

Beware of ever believing that anything is 100 per cent safe because that in itself leads to complacency and becomes a potential danger.

Using public transport

This is the cheapest but unfortunately the most problematical to organize. Secondary pupils are usually mature enough to be trusted to behave responsibly on buses or trains. In some cases, secondary pupils over 16 can make their own way to the venue, with written permission from their parents. I once worked in a special school where finding their way safely to the venue and back was part of the syllabus for citizenship.

Primary age pupils need reminders about behaviour and safety before you leave and lots of supervision en route. The following tips may help to make it run smoothly.

Safety
- When you cross a road always have an adult on the road to supervise if the pupils are walking in a crocodile.
- Always use pedestrian crossings and pelican lights on busy city roads, even if it means walking further.
- Some LEAs have a rule that the pupils must line up on the kerb and everyone cross together, with an adult at each end. This is sensible because it minimizes the time taken for everyone to cross.
- Count the heads twice before you go and every time you get off or on a bus or train.

- Designate one adult to be the last on and last off the bus or train. This ensures that you do not leave anyone behind.
- Warn the pupils that if they do get left behind on a bus or train, to go to the next station/bus stop, get off and wait on the platform or kerb until you come for them. This is another reason to have extra adult helpers. You should miss them straight away if you count the heads as soon as you get off the bus or train.

Organization

- Find out who in the class is likely to be travel sick. Telephone their parents and recommend that they give their children travel sickness pills before they leave the house, and ask them to give the welfare assistant/first-aider one for the journey back.
- Divide and rule. Allocate a written list of a small group to each adult to supervise and regularly count. It's easier for each adult to count six or seven, than to rely on yourself to count 30 or more.
- Always put the pupils with medication into the first-aider's group.
- If you work in a city school, never travel in the rush hour. I used to wait outside the Tube station with the class until a minute after the deadline time. It's also cheaper then, as well as more comfortable.
- Where possible buy the tickets in advance. It saves queuing and avoids pupils becoming restless while waiting.

What do you bring with you?

Personnel

- More helpers than the school policy demands.
- A member of staff who has completed a first-aid course. It is worth doing the course yourself. It's four days off school and has to be renewed every three years. It's useful because you don't have to go looking for a first-aider every time you want to go on a trip.
- An adult who doesn't mind cleaning up after a child has been sick.

Equipment

- The first-aid kit and pupils' medication. This is usually brought by the first-aider or welfare assistant.
- Sick bags, rubber gloves, small bottle of disinfectant, a few old newspapers to wrap up the sick bags before discarding them and a bottle of water. Never underestimate their importance.
- A cheap old perfume. If all else fails and a child is sick, spray it over the vomit to kill the smell so that it won't make you or anyone else sick, before it is cleaned up.
- A list of all the pupils' names and parents' home telephone and mobile numbers, in case a child falls ill or has an accident and needs to be rushed to hospital.
- A few extra vegetarian sandwiches. There is usually someone who forgets their packed lunch and hungry pupils are more bother in the afternoon.
- Extra money, in case something unforeseen happens and you need to pay for a taxi, suntan lotion, anything.
- Clipboards and pens/pencils, sharpeners, rubbers, worksheets.
- Drinks, and even biscuits perhaps, for the end of the journey if it's a long one.
- The school camera. Digital is best so you can run off dozens of pictures. Pupils are always more keen to write about something if they have a photo of themselves beside it. They also like to keep the picture to illustrate their work.
- Black bin liners to clear up all the mess after the packed lunch.
- Sanitary towels, if taking girls in Year 5 upwards.

Travelling on a hired coach

This is usually expensive but much simpler.

- Check beforehand that there are seatbelts and make sure every one is belted up before you move off.
- If a pupil refuses, have him/her excluded from the trip. If a pupil refuses to belt up on the way home and it's too late to exclude him/her from the trip, sit beside the little gem with your hand clamped over the inserted belt buckle and ignore all the protestations about you having no right to infringe his/her freedom of movement. (I have done it twice.)

- Make sure you exclude the bugger from the next trip and when his/her parents object, point out that it's for his/her own safety.
- Make sure the windows are shut and the coach air-conditioning is on. If the driver is unhelpful, tell him that it stops the pupils from being sick. They never argue after that.
- If the coach has no air-conditioning, open every window. Explain the advantages of avoiding food regurgitation if the driver objects.
- When you return, ask one of the helpers on the coach to scout around and check that everything has been removed from it. It saves you contacting coach companies to retrieve items left behind.

When you return

The following are important.

Personnel
- If the head agrees, tip the coach driver, if s/he has been helpful. Your school may need to use the company again.
- Stay with the pupils until the last one has been collected, unless they are old enough to go home alone.
- Personally thank each individual helper. It is vital to keep their goodwill because you are bound to need them again. Sometimes it's appropriate to invite them into the staffroom for a cup of tea, or your classroom if there is a policy not to have them in the staffroom.
- As a courtesy let the head know that everyone is back safely.

Equipment
- Grab all the clipboards and worksheets. The pupils will be too excited to remember them.
- Download the photos from the digital camera, or ask the ICT teacher or a smart pupil to do it for you.
- If using an ordinary camera you can order an extra set for only about £2 more. It's not much more costly than digital, as colour inkjet printers are very expensive.

- Email a note of thanks to anyone at the venue who has been helpful.

Suggested follow-up work

Of course it depends on the age of the pupils and this is by no means a finite list.

- Ask each group of pupils to write, or type, a letter of thanks to their group leader, telling them what they enjoyed most about the day and to anyone at the venue who made it an enjoyable day. This can be done by email. The pupils often prefer it and it's just as effective.
- Make a class book or large display about the day. Include pupils' own drawings, downloaded photos or even pictures cut out of leaflets or from the Internet.
- Make their own individual books about the day, using resources suggested in the last point. Pupils often prefer these because they can take it home as a souvenir afterwards.
- Ask the pupils to write down questions about the trip. Make a list and ask the pupils in groups to find the answers using the Internet, encyclopaedias and reference books. Have a session of reporting back to the class. Pupils often love this because it gives them the chance to play the part of the teacher.
- Use the day as a basis for your next class assembly. It saves you having to think up an idea and it reinforces what the pupils have learnt. If you plan this in advance it's worth having a set of slides, photos on PowerPoint or downloaded digital photographs to illustrate it.

All of this might make day trips sound time consuming and tedious. Fortunately you'll be broken in gently as someone more senior will do the organizing for you in your induction year. In later years, you'll become accustomed to the procedures and hopefully have the pleasure of seeing how your effort has enhanced the quality of education for your pupils and improved their attitude and standard of work.

8 Report writing

I have never heard of anyone being taught to write reports at college, although it's an important task, which takes up many hours of your time each year.

Many schools have computerized their reports so each teacher is provided with a floppy disk containing a string of comments for each subject, so you only have to delete the inapplicable and edit the rest. This makes the task wonderfully simple.

If you're lucky enough to be in that position, a good idea is to complete all of one gender, then the other, so that you don't have to keep replacing 'he' with 'she' and 'him' with 'her', etc. Another is to start with the most able, for whom there are fewer deletions to be made and then superimposing the next most able child's report on top of it, and so on, so you don't have to keep on deleting all the same sentences each time.

In secondary schools some subject teachers write four or five different reports of a few sentences each and select the most appropriate for each child so they only have to type in the name each time and perhaps change a few words or a sentence.

In other schools the teachers receive disks with blank skeleton reports, in which to type their comments. I find it easiest to type the first report, copy and paste it on to a similar child's report and then start editing the details. It is very important to read the first one a few times before you start copying and pasting it, because if you make a mistake you have to correct it on every report.

Again type all of one gender first to avoid using the wrong pronouns. With some subjects, for example PE, RE, ICT, it's appropriate to type a few sentences outlining the topics studied, cut and paste it onto each report and then add a paragraph about the individual's personal progress.

Each of the above is a superb way to cut the labour to a

minimum, although the comments have to be edited carefully if they are to be accurate and informative to the parents. If you have twins in your class, make sure their reports are not absolutely identical.

Try to avoid using the words 'good', 'well' and 'bad'. They are boring words and you can usually find a more descriptive one. Your report writing will look and sound much more professional if you use interesting, thoughtful expressions like the ones below:

Positive comments which parents like to read

- contributes sensibly;
- shows clear understanding;
- takes a pride in;
- listens attentively;
- likes to take part in;
- lively imagination;
- sound general knowledge;
- has a wide range of interests;
- always tries his/her best;
- is quick to take in new information;
- has an efficient memory for;
- is well organized/fluent/responsible/enthusiastic;
- sensible/careful worker/continues to improve;
- retains facts easily;
- able to grasp concepts easily;
- applies him/herself sensibly to all areas of the curriculum;
- joins in all activities enthusiastically;
- enjoys lessons;
- continues to progress and develop.

The word 'average' is currently out of vogue and many teachers react – I sometimes think over-react – to it. I think these are better:

- works well with the middle range of the class;
- can keep up with at least half of the class;
- can work independently, although s/he does not rise to the top of the class.

Negative comments

It is much easier to write a positive report than a negative one. Parents are often upset by negative comments on a report. In some cases it can cause embarrassing arguments and I have even known cases where parents have wanted comments removed. The trick is to find a positive way of telling the negative truth without causing offence.

I think these work well.

For the less able
- slow but steady;
- tries hard but has difficulty with;
- puts in great effort but lacks confidence/concentration;
- puts in effort but can be careless;
- needs lots of practice at each level;
- copes best in a small group;
- needs regular practice of basic skills.

For the unenthusiastic
- his/her inability to concentrate is having an adverse effect on his/her own progress and that of others;
- sometimes makes avoidable mistakes;
- needs to take more care with;
- needs to be treated firmly to stay on task;
- needs to put in more effort to keep up with the group;
- often needs to finish off his/her work at break times.

For the child with poor social skills
- has some difficulty in making and keeping friends;
- does not yet understand how his/her behaviour effects other pupil's reactions to him/her;
- does not always respect other pupil's space;
- must learn that a glib answer or giving back-chat will not get him/her what s/he wants.

It is never wise to write anything pernicious on a report however much you feel it may be true or justifiable. Remember these reports stay in a file for years and it hardly seems fair that someone should be reading something awful about a child several years later. Some say that reports should be written on paper which self-destructs after about five years. I'm inclined to agree with that.

If there's anything very unpleasant to tell, I always say to the parents on consultation evening, 'I haven't written this down for people in the future to pick up and read. I prefer to just tell parents quietly in private that . . . ' Put like that, parents are more likely to accept it and they appreciate a teacher's keeping their child's worst attributes private.

The most difficult part is writing under the headings 'Behaviour', 'Personality', and 'Personal qualities'. Again the problematical part is writing the unvarnished truth without making it sound like a character defamation. The suggestions below are for extreme cases only.

A few useful euphemisms

Euphemism for the report	Meaning
only responds positively to very firm handling	is spoilt/badly brought up
is inconsiderate of other pupils' feelings	is spiteful
provokes other pupils	is always causing fights
is a verbose child	never shuts up
seeks a lot of attention in class	never gives me a moment's peace
has difficulty in sharing a teacher/ resources with others	is selfish
misleads others/we are unable to trust his word	tells lies
is often confused between fact and fantasy	often tells lies
misleads adults and pupils to others' disadvantage	tells malicious lies
does not distinguish between his own and other people's property	steals

Euphemism for the report	Meaning
lacks moral awareness	lies, cheats and steals
does not show respect to adults	is infuriatingly cheeky
is a reluctant scholar	is lazy as sin
frequently has to finish work at play/PE times	is often lazy as sin
uses inappropriate vocabulary	effs and blinds like a drunken fishwife
threatens the safety of other pupils	is downright vicious
relates better to younger pupils	is immature and ought to act his age
does not respond to either sanction or counselling	needs a shrink

Getting the tone right as well as getting the information across accurately is the most important part. If this is your first year or you're new to the school, don't worry about having a reaction from the parents, because all reports are ultimately the responsibility of the head. After you have written them, the head must read and sign each one. That signature represents his/her approval, so if there's any objections from parents, the head must support you.

This task is very time consuming and tedious, and unfortunately often has to be done in the latter half of each term when teachers are more tired or already encumbered with other tasks, like marking examination papers. As soon as you receive your report sheets or floppy disks, it is wise to start them straightaway. I like to work out how many I should do per night to finish with a week to spare. Those teachers who leave it to the last minute end up working until two in the morning and giving a poor performance in class or irritating their colleagues by taking a sickie when everyone knows why.

Be kind to yourself. When you've finished, reward yourself with a night out, or if you have children of your own take them on some non-educational trip to compensate them for neglecting them while you've been struggling through all the extra typing.

9 The politics of the staffroom

Who's your friend?

The politics of the staffroom can be an unholy business. I have known one mature person who, after doing her placement in a primary school where the atmosphere was particularly unpleasant, decided to withdraw from a PGCE course, and an experienced teacher who resigned and took three part-time jobs to avoid it. You can preserve your sanity and survive more gracefully by staying out of staffroom politics as long as you can.

The staff are like the head's class. An even-handed, kindly and efficient teacher usually has a happy, united and hard-working class and the same applies to the head and the staff. Of course there are many excellent heads who can take a widely differing group of teachers and mould them into a happy, united and effective team. If you're fortunate enough to be in a school like this, then you may not need all the advice in this chapter.

Factions in the staffroom

When the staffroom has factions in it, not only do the pupils sense it and exploit the situation by getting through the cracks, but the more aggressive and power-happy teachers do so as well. Strong heads keep a staff united by their own even-handedness and refusal to give ears to any teacher criticizing or complaining about another. Some weak heads feel threatened by a united staff and consciously or unconsciously set about creating divisions. I have known schools where the staff could be divided into two or three groups: those in favour with the hierarchy, those not and those who are ignored by the hierarchy.

If you're in a school with factions, it's important to keep quiet at least until you've worked out who is in each clique. Even then, it's still usually best to stay out of all of them. This ensures you have no enemies, but it may also mean that you have no close friends on the staff. Staffrooms can be divided on lots of issues like:

- those who support the head and those who don't;
- those who want the school to use more modern techniques and those who prefer a traditional approach to everything;
- those who encourage more parent power and those who like to marginalize the parents.

Whatever the issue that divides the staff, it's best never to comment on it at all. Nor is it wise to try steering a mid-path between two factions who want to move in opposite directions. People who walk up the middle of a road get knocked down by cars going in both directions.

Staffroom sneaks

Even in your second year it's sensible not to comment negatively on anything in the school unless in private and you are certain you can trust the person to whom you're speaking. Some heads have a supergrass – a teacher who sits in the staffroom quietly listening in to everyone's conversation and then reporting it back to the head. To test out a suspected supergrass, I used to pick up the *TES* and comment to her about available jobs. After two such occasions, I was summoned to the office and asked if I was looking for a new job.

It is safest to listen quietly to people who moan to you, but don't enter into the conversation until you know whom you can trust not to repeat your comments, and who likes running to the head to drop you in it. There is nothing worse than telling one of your peers what you dislike about the head and then discovering that s/he is having an affair with him/her.

Some teachers watch their colleagues and report them to the head for any misdemeanors – losing/breaking a piece of equipment, coming in late, etc. Some say one thing when the head is present and the opposite when s/he is not.

If you have any of the above in your school, it's better to stay well away from all of them. Sometimes young teachers are tempted to cultivate their friendship as they are seen as safe company.

Any friendship which these teachers offer is superficial, can be withdrawn at any time and frequently is.

The doom and gloom lot

A minute number of teachers have very negative attitudes and are constantly moaning. Worse, they generate a negative attitude which can grow and spoil a happy atmosphere. I always smile, say good morning and move on. Keeping your morale up is vital to being able to enthuse pupils and stay on top of the job, and these people can depress you.

Getting personal

At the end of term staff party, it's sensible to avoid anyone who has any power, and avoid the sickening feeling of waking up the next morning and remembering what you said while under the influence.

Occasionally, heads and deputies conduct romantic liaisons with a member of staff. You can suss it out by the extra confident swagger they suddenly acquire, or the over-zealous manner in which one defends the other when they're challenged. This causes consternation among the staff, because great powershifts ensue. It causes no problem if one of them leaves, or they at least conduct themselves in an impeccably careful manner.

Sometimes the member of staff takes advantage of his or her new-found status and power and is duly resented. Tension and acrimony erupt and spread like tremors of an earthquake. It is safest to avoid all discussion of the matter except with your most trusted friends because gossip often returns to its subject. It is never wise to pass on anyone's comments because teachers who do so are never trusted again.

The powershift

The most difficult time to cope with staff politics is during the first two years of a new head. A powershift means that some people go up, some go down and someone gets hurt. Teachers who were in favour with the previous head can lose their influence under the new one and suffer the indignity of finding that their status is severely undermined. If this happens to you, you've two choices, grin and bear it or leave. Staying and fighting to recover your influence is not an option. I knew a teacher who tried it, and her influence and respect from the staff disintegrated daily.

Some new heads manage to gain the respect and goodwill of their staff within a few weeks. Some drive out most of the staff in two years. Heads who lack confidence begin by populating the staffroom with their own friends from past schools. This often builds up a 'them' and 'us' atmosphere which can be so severe that teachers leave, even though they themselves are not being harassed. This in turn exacerbates the situation, because the head can then employ more of his/her own pals. It is best to keep your head down in these circumstances. Try not to be associated with either group, especially the clique who are congregating around the head, because their friendship is usually quite shallow and association earns you the distrust of the rest of the staff.

The worst possible situation is when a teacher has used his or her influence and favour with the head to attack others. I knew one such teacher and, under a new head, he went straight out of favour while one of his former victims found favour and wreaked his vengeance. What goes around, comes around. There is a God.

There might be a teacher who bears grudges for months and even years and these are best avoided like a wasps' nest. It is never wise to let irritations stay with you because schools are heavily pressurized communities and mountains grow out of molehills if not smoothed over.

Large schools are easier to work in than small ones, because in a large building it's easier to avoid anyone whom you find difficult company.

All of this may be painting a dismal picture. This is not the aim. Many schools have a happy, friendly atmosphere, with a terrific head and mutually-supportive teachers who keep each other afloat and laughing through every pitfall and challenge.

10 Don't forget the big picture

In the hurly-burly of every busy day, it can become easy to lose sight of the real world. It's a bit like being a housewife. The more hours you put into the job, the more you notice there is to do.

When heads want a job done, they tend to ask the busy members of staff. Some teachers, driven by an innate, creative urge, or just eagerness to succeed, become carried away and spend so much time on the job, they become too tired to enjoy anything outside work. Some fall victim to the 'willing horse' syndrome. Heads spot the most efficient and ambitious teachers and give them a disproportionally large burden of extra tasks. Don't fall for it. Learn to use the word 'no'. Of course you can dress it up a bit with answers like:

- 'Sorry, I'm snowed under with . . . '
- 'Sorry, I really can't take on anything extra until I have finished . . . '
- 'Sorry, for the moment I really must make it my priority to . . . '

Your mind needs to escape from work to stay sane and allow you to return to school refreshed. I was most impressed when a young teacher, about to go abroad, told me that in his new school, teachers were encouraged to have an interesting hobby which had nothing to do with their work. I'm sure it would enhance the quality of life for all teachers if UK schools adopted the same view.

You might join a night class of some activity you enjoy, preferably one which is totally different from work. Unless for something unavoidable like parents' night, try never to miss it because of school work.

It is worthwhile to stay in touch with past college friends, even if they're at the other end of the country. If they're teachers you can encourage each other. Some teachers go home late, feeling so tired their social life gradually starts to disintegrate during the term time, especially the first term.

However busy you might be, making new friends ought to be a priority, especially if you've moved to a different part of the country. If you go out for an evening with colleagues, try not to spend too much time talking about school. You'll feel better afterwards if you have stimulated your brain with something else.

One way to keep your spirits up is always to have some little treat to which you can look forward, a trip to the theatre or cinema, a game of football, a massage or just a night in the pub.

If you think that working 50 or more hours per week is unreasonable for an NQT's salary, remember that your body and mind will adjust to the long hours and the following year will be much easier. It's comforting to realize that stress levels usually subside in the second year because you know the ropes and are no longer worried you may not pass your induction year.

When your induction year is over

When you reach the end of your first year and pass, make sure you don't do more than three or four days of school work during the holidays. A day at the beginning to sort out your classroom and two or three days just before you return for the Inset days at the start of the new term is plenty.

Now is the time to reward yourself with a comfortable and relaxing, or exciting, holiday. It puts everything into perspective and reminds you that there's more to life than work. It also gives you the strength to face the next year and a taste of how you would like to spend your holidays in the future.

Remember, we are now living in an age where the world is your oyster and teachers with their long summer holidays can take advantage of it more than most. You've had the stress and hard work. Now's the time to make up for it and spoil yourself. It is teaching's big advantage over other occupations. You'll be amazed how uplifted you will feel after a few weeks of doing something completely different.

Some teachers get into gear as soon as the pupils disappear on the last afternoon and others return the day before, or even hours before, the start of term. In some staffrooms the conversation sounds like it's a travel agent's shop at the end of term.

There are a number of companies which specialize in a huge variety of summer adventures. Key into www.exodus.co.uk and find a trip for every exotic taste. There are holidays touring the east coast of Australia – snorkling, exploring the Great Barrier Reef, sailing, white water rafting or quad-biking. You can explore India's historic sites, its magical temples and idyllic beaches.

Try these websites:

- www.JourneyLatinAmerica.co.uk
- www.worldexpeditions.co.uk
- www.magictravel.co.uk

There are heaps more in the travel section of *The Sunday Times*. And remember they apply all year round. You could have white Christmas and New Year holidays skiing in Bulgaria, the Pyrenees or the Dolomites. It's all there ready for the taking.

I have worked with teachers of all ages who have joined the Ramblers and found that going off in an unfamiliar group was a great way to drive all thoughts of education out of their heads and return them to their classrooms full of energy and enthusiasm to face the challenges of another year.

Remember that Easyjet (www.easyjet.co.uk) and Ryanair (www.ryanair.co.uk) both do cheap flights, even during holiday times, so think ahead and book up well in advance. Once the trip is booked it'll make the light at the end of the tunnel larger and closer.

And of course when you do return to the grindstone you might like to seek out the NQTs in your school, make them welcome and offer them some friendly support and encouragement.

Part Two

How to make the most of the next thirty years

11 Getting promotions

A friend once jokingly said to me, 'There are two types of teachers, those who know where they're going, and I don't care much for their destination; and the rest of us'.

Many teachers enjoy the interaction of the classroom, the creative pleasure it gives them and the satisfaction of seeing progress in their pupils' work, attitude and behaviour so much, that they're content to stay there. Being unambitious is not a weakness. Many such teachers are highly competent, give their schools stability, and are just as valuable to the profession as those who climb the promotion ladder.

However, the profession also needs teachers who are ambitious and want to develop a wide range of skills, inside and outside the classroom, to be the next generation of heads, advisors, advanced skills teachers and inspectors. Gaining a promotion improves one's status and income and leads gradually out of the classroom and into the office. Some teachers look for promotion simply because they need the money, while others want to climb the ladder of success for their own fulfilment. If you're ambitious, have vision and want to be a head, inspector, advisor or an advanced skills teacher, early promotion is advisable.

Looking for the next job

It is best to wait until you've completed your first two terms and start feeling confident that you'll survive the induction year. Then start casting your eye around for future professional development. Decide what you're best at and mention to the head that you will eventually look for a post in that area. A head who wants to keep you might comment that s/he may have something in that area or another one. If you're in a secondary school teaching one or two subjects, say that you would like to take on some extra responsibility next year. Unfortunately s/he might refer you to the *Times Educational Supplement* (*TES*) jobs section or ignore the comment, in which case, don't be disheartened because most teachers who want a post of responsibility, eventually acquire one.

As soon as you start your second year, become active. Start going on courses in the area for which you would like a post of responsibility, preferably during school time. It is harder to get maximum benefit from twilight courses because everyone is so tired after a day's work, and a trek across town to the Teachers' Centre can be too much. Afterwards, write up a précis of the course and circulate it round the staff in the next staff meeting.

Wherever your talent lies, start an after-school club in that area. Many schools have extra-curricular clubs for drama, art, choir, dance, football, ICT and a host of other subjects. Although one should never run a club in one's induction year because there are too many other pressures, there are great advantages in doing so in later years. It helps build up a stronger and more positive relationship with the pupils and this spills over into the classroom. Heads appreciate the value of it and even if they don't offer you a post, it will certainly go on your reference.

Don't hang around forever hoping for the offer of an extra increment in return for added responsibility. If the head has not offered one by the end of the Easter term in your second year, start looking in the *TES*. The easiest way is to visit their website www.tes.co.uk and click in to 'TESjobs'. You might also try www.eteach.com. Always tell your head when you see a post for which you intend to apply. They appreciate the courtesy. Many are annoyed when they first hear about it from the head who applies to them for a reference.

If the head advertises a suitable post on the staff notice board, make sure you study the job description carefully. Be wary of expressions like 'any other task which the head deems appropriate'. It covers a multitude of related and unrelated tasks and it's worth asking what it means. Whether you apply for a post in your own or another school, you have to go through the procedure of application and interview.

If you decide to apply for a post in a successful school in an attractive area, you may have to fight off a fair bit of competition just to be offered an interview. If you apply for a post in a challenging school, it's easier to acquire one but, of course, the demands are greater when you get it.

The preliminary visit

Before you visit look on the school's website, but treat it as a holiday brochure or an estate agent's leaflet. Only the best side of the school will be depicted on it.

As with applying for your first job, always telephone and ask to come and see the school if it's in the state sector. Most heads want to meet applicants before the interview and many are sizing them up in preparation for shortlisting. The impression you make at this point is important because there's a definite element of subjectivity about the process. Heads only shortlist teachers whom they like, they believe will fit in with the rest of the staff and form a positive relationship with the pupils.

Some heads, who have lots of applicants, will tell you to wait until the day of the interview, but I have not yet met a state school head who will shortlist a teacher who has not at least asked for a visit. Private school heads take a different stance and will shortlist purely on application form or CV and letter of application.

By this time you'll be fairly confident and not find the procedure as nerve-wracking as you may have done the first time round. While trying to make a favourable impression on the head, try and find out a few pieces of useful information for yourself.

What to look for
- Noise levels. Always visit during lesson time and make sure you're shown around the school. Check the noise levels in classrooms. Is it a busy, productive sound or excessive and plain rowdy?
- Classroom behaviour. Are the pupils on task, polite and reasonably interested in their work?
- Playground behaviour. It is also worth looking out to see if there are any fights in the playground. I would consider these a higher priority than SATs/GCE results, although it is, of course, worth looking at those as well.
- What the job demands. Remember this is a two-way process.

Teachers often forget that they need to assess whether the school is right for them. A considerate headteacher will try to give you plenty of information about everything which the job requires and allow you a chance to ask questions.

- Atmosphere. Try to assess whether the school has a happy, welcoming atmosphere. For me, this is more important than a high place on the league tables.

- Ask the annual rate of staff turnover. If it's a low percentage rate, it's an encouraging sign, because unless there's a shortage of jobs, teachers won't stay in a school if it's not a pleasant, happy place. If the turnover is high, the head may resent your asking, but it doesn't matter because it probably isn't a school where you would want to work anyway.

- Behaviour policy. As you walk around the school look out for charts with pupil's names, stars and stickers. Ask the head what incentive schemes and reward systems they use. It's sensible for a school to have a few positive ways of encouraging pupils, but if they have lots of them, tread carefully because that usually means the pupils are difficult to motivate and there are difficulties with behaviour management.

- Parking space. Don't underestimate its importance. It's annoying to find yourself in an inner-city school with no on-site or street parking, so you have to use public transport, which may add an hour's tedium to each end of your working day.

- The stock rooms. Are they open for the staff to enter at will or are they locked and staff can only take out resources once per week under supervision? In my experience, these schools have a lower level of trust between staff and management.

- Name policy. It is best not to address the head by their first name until you're sure it's acceptable. In a few schools the staff are still not allowed to do so. In others, the pupils address the staff, even the head, by their first names. This can be important to some teachers, who have strong feelings on the subject.

- Lunchtime arrangements. In a state school you cannot theoretically be forced to eat in the dining hall with the pupils and the noise but occasionally pressure is put on teachers to do so. It can give you a headache after a frustrating morning and leave you less fit for the afternoon's challenges. You could find out if they give you a free lunch if you eat there. Is the food edible? In private schools it can be compulsory to eat with the pupils but often worth it, as you're compensated with a tasty free lunch.

- The extra clauses. Check what overnight school journeys you'll have to go on, and if there are any Saturday commitments.

- Would you feel comfortable with the school's standards of dress? Most heads dislike teachers dressing in extremes of fashion, although you may find a school where it's tolerated. In some schools teachers aren't allowed to wear denim and men have to wear a tie. You really have no choice but to accept the school's ruling or look elsewhere.

The letter of application

Most LEAs have a standard application form of about four sides of A4. As with the form for your first job, photocopy the form and fill it in, in pencil, to make sure you have every detail correct. It usually says 'use black ink' to fill in the original. It is quite straightforward except for the blank page which asks you to write your supporting information. Writing an interesting and impressive letter of application can be vital for getting an interview. I have heard that some heads like brief letters and only read the first page. I ignore that because heads who only read the first page seem unappreciative of teachers' efforts and I would not want to work with them.

First of all, look at the job description. Some are brief and to the point, but some are two to three pages long. Be guided by the length of it. A long job description needs a lengthy detailed letter.

Always type the letter, unless asked for a handwritten one, and if necessary staple it to the form. Every item on the job description must be dealt with in the letter, because some heads make a list of items and tick them off as they read the letters. Some even have a system of awarding a number of points for each item and shortlisting the applicants who score the highest number.

This is the letter plan which has always worked well for me in the past.

Study the job description carefully and make a list of all the items to be included and number each one. For example,

1   Ability to work amicably in a team.
2   Ability to cope with a wide range of abilities.
3   Ability to form positive relationships with parents.
4   Sympathy for underprivileged pupils.
5   Flexibility.
6   Ability to work with a range of age groups.
7   Willingness to take part in educational visits and school journeys.
8   Extra-curricular activities you can offer.
9   Innovations for which you have been responsible.
10 In-service education for teachers (Inset) you have delivered to staff.
11 Inset which you have attended.
12 Sense of humour.

The list can sometimes stretch to 30 items. Next, make a plan for the letter. The plan might look something like this.

1   Introductory sentence naming the post and its reference number. This is necessary because some heads advertise several posts in the same week. Add a summary sentence about yourself.
2   Paragraph about each job and post you've had so far, giving a longer description of each.
3   Paragraphs about how you view the post advertised and why you think you are suitable for it.
4   Paragraph about extra-curricular activities.
5   Some paragraphs about your own philosophy of education.
6   Paragraph about your own interests outside school.
7   Final enthusiastic sentence.

Next, go down the list of items to be included and put its number beside a paragraph on the letter plan, to ensure that nothing is omitted. As with the letter for the first job, the tone of the letter is as important as the content. If you are stuck for ideas try some of the expressions below.

Introductory paragraph
I submit the following in support of my application for the post of . . . in Gasworks Primary School, as advertised in the *Times*

Educational Supplement, 13th April, ref. no. G352. I have been a teacher for seven years and held posts of responsibility for maths and history.

Paragraphs about each job you've had
Name and describe each post and say how you've developed that subject in your school. Make it clear you appreciate the experience and show how it has made you a better teacher. If you have never had a post of responsibility before, say so, but add all the extra things you have done for your school – run an after-school club, helped backstage with the school play, driven pupils to their football/netball matches, etc.

Use expressions like:

- 'In this post I learnt . . . '
- 'I value this experience because . . . '
- 'This experience helped me to develop the skill of . . . '
- 'In this school I became interested in . . . '
- 'I acquired enormous job satisfaction from . . . '

Paragraphs about how you envisage the post advertised
Describe how you would go about fulfilling the post, adding details of any relevant Inset courses you've attended and how they helped you gain necessary expertise. Describe all your skills. Mention any extra qualifications which you possess, for example, Special Needs diploma, Open University credits, NOF certificate for computer training or a first-aid certificate. If you acquired any qualifications while working full-time, make sure you say so. It shows added dedication to the job and usually impresses the head.

Paragraphs on your philosophy of education
Include sentences like:

- 'I believe in teaching pupils to love books/learn new skills . . . '
- 'I like pupils to appreciate the value of . . . '
- 'I believe that we must teach pupils to respect each other because . . . '
- 'For me the hidden curriculum is important because . . . '

Use plenty of righteousness and moral rectitude. Heads love it!

Final enthusiastic sentence

Try one of these:

- 'I view this post as an exciting chance to extend the skills I have developed in teaching.'
- 'I should love to have this post as it would give me the opportunity to use the skills I acquired on a course on . . . '
- 'I should view this post as an interesting challenge.'

Never say in the letter that you intend using the post as a jumping off point to something higher up the ladder.

Organizational points

Always keep a skeleton letter of application on your computer (or on a floppy disk, if you've used someone else's computer) so you don't have to type it out every time you apply for a post. If you're not invited to an interview at first, and have to apply for several, it's efficient to print the skeleton letter out on scrap paper, go through it in minute detail and cross out all the information that is irrelevant and add anything needed. Then edit the original.

Save each individual letter under its own file name. This saves effort because you might apply for a post with a similar job description to a previous one. Even when you have found a post, do not delete the files. In three years' time you may find them useful when you apply for the next one.

The interview

Start preparing answers to the following questions, as applicable to the post you're applying for.

- Why are you interested in this post?
- What attracts you to this school?
- What qualifications/special qualities can you bring to this post?
- How do you view the role of the coordinator for ICT/music/technology?
- How would you develop ICT/netball/music further within the school?
- What items would you include in the school policy for ICT?

- How would you advise teachers whom you felt could improve their performance in this area?
- How would you assess pupils' progress in this area?
- How would you spend your budget for this post?
- Our SATs/GCSE/A-level results are low. How would you go about improving them?
- If offered the post, would you accept it?

Prepare detailed answers and write out the questions and answers in the days leading up to the interview. Read them about an hour before the interview and try not to be in the classroom during the two hours prior to the interview, because you'll perform better with a clear head, and not feel irritated by some classroom incident.

Ask your partner/friend to give you a practice interview the night before, asking the questions for you to regurgitate your notes. Don't make up your mind about the final question until you're asked it. Sometimes people change their mind during the interview.

Dress smartly, hold your head up, your shoulders back and look the interview panel in the eyes and smile.

If you don't hit the target on your first throw

Don't be disheartened if you don't find a post quickly, because many teachers attend several interviews. Don't look upon it as a failure, but as worthwhile practice for future interviews.

For any post where you're not successful or don't get shortlisted, always ring up the head and ask why not. A tactful way of putting it is, 'Thank you for your letter. It would be very helpful to me for the future if you could give me some feedback as to why you decided against me'.

Heads expect applicants to ask and in my experience are very helpful. Sometimes they say you did nothing wrong, you were a close second and if they had another post, would be pleased to hear from you. Sometimes they tell you about mistakes you made and if this is the case, don't feel hurt. This is useful information which will help you in the future. You can take at face value any positive remarks they make because they really won't encourage you if they don't think you deserved it, not least because they won't want to have the bother of dealing with another application from you if they really don't want you.

The next step

When you have fulfilled your post successfully for a couple of years, change and try another one, because you are more likely to go to the top with a wide range of experience. If you are unambitious and only want a post for the extra money, try to hold on to the same post as long as you can, so you don't have to waste precious leisure hours on writing another policy, organizing assessment procedures, ordering resources and overhauling the curriculum in a new area. In many cases, a post of responsibility becomes easier to handle the longer you have it.

When you step onto the greasy pole

If you are ambitious, keep an eye on the future. There are now more career opportunities for competent, enthusiastic teachers than in recent decades. In order to progress, it's wise to start building up a staff profile. The more supportive heads actually provide teachers with blank portfolios and details of what to put in them. Items include:

- job descriptions you have fulfilled;
- additional certificates and diplomas;
- a list of all the Inset courses you have attended and the précis which you delivered back to the staff;
- details of Inset you delivered to the staff;
- copies of all the monitoring feedback on your observed lessons;
- evidence of planning and feedback;
- evidence of initiatives you have led at school;
- Ofsted grades;
- SATs, QCA, GCSE, AS-level and A-level results of your classes;
- action plans which you have organized and fulfilled for your posts of responsibility;
- school policies you have written;
- performance management targets which you have achieved;
- assessment procedures you have set up;
- photographs of school teams you have trained, dance groups you have trained, school trips and journey activities;

- itineraries and programmes of activities of school journeys you have organized or with which you have assisted;
- programmes of school plays, productions and concerts you have organized.

Get the filing cabinet filled

For later opportunities to proceed to higher pay scales remember we are now in the era of accountability, so it's important to start hoarding evidence of your competence and hard work. If you're planning to climb higher, it's well worth buying a filing cabinet if you did not get one at college, because in future years you will be required to produce a variety of pieces of evidence.

Keep a copy of all your paperwork at home – planning sheets, worksheets – especially if the head forbids you to remove any of it from the premises. If space is a problem, I have often found it easier to do all my plans and worksheets on my home computer, for easy storage and instant access.

And when you reach the top

The higher you go up the ladder, the more administrative work and the less teaching you do. This suits many teachers, but some gradually lose the skill of class teaching. A friend who is a head told me this can happen within a year or two of landing a headship, especially as classroom practice can change with alarming speed.

It is wise to keep the skill of class teaching if you become a head, deputy, senior member of staff or even a support teacher. Colleagues treat you with more respect if they know you can still confidently handle a difficult class, and smile behind their hands if they hear you trying to avoid being locked up alone with one.

12 Alternative options for promotion

After a few years of having posts of responsibility, you may feel ready for another step upwards. Many teachers are eager for promotion and go for the deputy head and headteacher route. A few have told me that headteacher is the only job they have ever really wanted. I have even known an NQT telling of his plans to be a deputy in five years and a head a few years after that.

Others want to progress but don't want to go down that route, because head and deputy are very stressful jobs and involve a vast number of extra hours of tedious administrative work and often don't give much creative pleasure or job satisfaction. There are other career routes for competent, ambitious teachers who want to progress.

Figure 1 is a Career Tree to show some of the routes to advancing your career.

Of course you need not follow the routes shown exactly. On rare occasions teachers have become heads without being deputies first, or become inspectors without being headteachers first. This may change in the future as today you need to complete the headteachers' course and pass its assignments before applying for a headship.

Now is a chance to look at the other options and what they entail. I shall explore those highlighted in the following three chapters.

Advisory teachers/consultants. Who are they? what do they do?

An advisory teacher or consultant is highly skilled in one area of the curriculum or one key stage. They are not assigned to any particular school and can be based at LEA offices or Teachers' Centres. Every LEA has a team of primary and secondary advisory teachers or

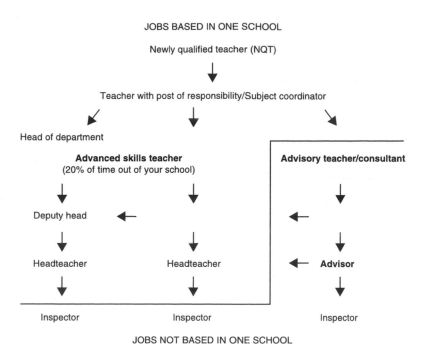

Figure 1 Career tree showing alternative routes for promotion

consultants, normally one or two per subject. Some employ advisory teachers or consultants for age ranges, such as early years, and in recent years LEAs have begun employing advisory teachers to liaise with the voluntary and independent sector.

It is an advisory teacher's job to advise teachers on how to provide top quality lessons and to support their professional development. Their clients are the LEA's teachers rather than the pupils.

For more information see Chapter 13.

What does an advisor do?

This post is a step up from being an advisory teacher. An advisor is a highly skilled and experienced teacher who has moved beyond the classroom into management of certain curriculum areas throughout the whole LEA. Advisors are not attached to any one school and are normally based at the LEA offices.

This is an advantageous jumping-off post if you want to move on to a headship. They work closely with advisory teachers and consultants and their roles vary depending on the size of the LEA. Their tasks include inspecting and monitoring schools' progress and running courses for teachers and other school staff.

For more information see Chapter 14.

Advanced skills teachers (ASTs). Who are they? What do they do?

Advanced skills teachers are primary or secondary teachers who have demonstrated excellence in almost every area of their job.

The function of an AST is to advise and support other teachers and spread their expertise around to help others improve.

For more information see Chapter 15.

13 Advisory teacher/consultant

What do they do?

This can vary from one LEA to another. Their tasks include:

- organizing courses for teachers at the Teachers' Centre;
- visiting schools to give In-service education to teachers during their Inset days, or for shorter sessions such as staff meetings;
- giving demonstration lessons in class;
- scrutinizing how schools implement the National Curriculum in their subject area;
- observing how their subject is taught in schools, making a list of suggestions for improvement and helping the staff to implement them;
- supporting and advising teachers with lesson planning;
- introducing changes in the national and local policy in the teaching of their subject, for example literacy hour or numeracy hour;
- advising teachers on resourcing the school for their area of responsibility;
- organizing network meetings.

Advisory teachers work alongside other advisory teachers, consultants, advisors and inspectors.

Salary and pensions

Teachers are often seconded to be advisory teachers. This means that the job is advertised and any experienced teacher can apply for it. If appointed, they continue on the same salary that they would have had, if they had stayed in their school post. Sometimes they are transferred to another scale called Soulbury but the rise is not huge.

Sometimes, in the first instance, their posts are temporary for a fixed period like two years, and made permanent when the time is complete. I have known teachers to be in advisory posts for many years. The experience is an excellent jumping-off board for promotion to deputy head.

They either pay into the Teachers' Superannuation Scheme, the same pension scheme as class and subject teachers, or are transferred to the Local Government Scheme. It varies from one LEA to the next. You need to check all this out before applying.

What skills do you need?

Inter-personal skills

You need to be able to establish a positive working relationship with teachers and pupils quickly, because each class you teach is new to you so you're constantly breaking new ground.

Self-confidence not self-consciousness

Every single lesson is observed by one or more teachers/governors/ parents. You are held up as an expert, so there's a certain amount of pressure to deliver a tip-top lesson every time. You always have to give your observers an evaluation sheet so you are quickly told if you're not up to scratch. Unlike a class teacher you can never throw in the odd lesson at half-cock. It's a bit like having Ofsted all year.

Flexibility

Very important, because you're frequently working to someone else's agenda. A highly successful drama advisory teacher gave me an example. Two classes of nine year olds were experiencing difficulty in resolving conflicts without resorting to violence, especially at football. The staff wanted to do some team building and work on social skills and asked him to devise a drama lesson to support the project. A tall order to solve that one in an hour!

Boundless energy and enthusiasm

The job has long hours of contact because Inset often has to be delivered to teachers after school. The task is made doubly difficult because teachers are hard to motivate at evening sessions, since they're tired after being locked up with demanding classes all day. I once sat in an evening session with about 70 other teachers three days before the end of the Christmas term. I felt sorry for the guy who had prepared his talk meticulously well, and delivered it while we nodded off to sleep from sheer exhaustion.

An ability to pitch your lessons at every age range

You have to deliver Inset to a whole staff from nursery to Year 6, or Year 7 to Year 13. Whatever your subject, it can be hard to find topics which can be pitched at all levels, and invariably some teachers will feel outdone if you miss them out.

Level-headedness

On rare occasions you meet the teachers who think that people do the advisory job because it's an escape route from the classroom. This is hardly fair since in some ways it's much more difficult. One highly successful advisory teacher told me how she had prepared an Inset session and was met by a hostile group of teachers and who spent the time making cynical and rude remarks.

Two days in the life of an advisory teacher

You can see why you need the qualities above when you look at a couple of days in the life of an advisory teacher.

Monday

7.30am	Arrive at office and take messages off the answerphone and emails.
8.30am	Arrive at Dashwood Infants School to do partnership teaching lesson with NQT and Year 2 class.
9am	Do Year 2 lesson.
10.30am	Evaluate lesson with class teacher.
11.45am	Notify head of work done and discuss details for next Inset on target setting.
12.30pm	Arrive at Blank Lane Primary School to meet Year 5 teachers to discuss scheme of lessons for literacy hour.
1.30pm	Spend hour-long session in class observing Year 5 pupils. At playtime suggest plenary activities to class teacher.
2.30pm	Call in to see head and give an account of what we intend to do in the next six sessions in the class.

3.15pm   Return to Teachers' Centre to set up video and Power-
           Point display for NQT induction.
4.15pm   Deliver induction session.
5.45pm   Check everything is ready for tomorrow.
6.15pm   Go home.

Tuesday
7.30am   Arrive at office and take messages off the answerphone
           and emails.
8.00am   Meet another advisory teacher to plan in detail a session
           of Inset to be delivered to subject coordinators.
1pm   Meet senior members of staff at Faraway School at the
           other end of the borough to help them to prepare for
           their Ofsted inspection. Give them a list of issues which
           the inspectors will be checking, questions they are likely
           to be asked and discuss the types of classroom practice
           they are likely to be looking for. Check their planning
           system. Suggest improvements.
4pm   Arrive at Someother School to meet English coordin-
           ator to help him plan his next Inset session for the school
           staff.
5.30pm   Go home.

Qualifications and experience

Any experienced, competent teacher with all, or most, of the above
skills can apply for an advisory post. Although it is not absolutely
necessary, many advise having a substantial qualification, like an
MA in their subject, so that they are seen to have a large body of
knowledge which they can pass on to teachers. Others emphasize
the value of a long and wide experience to be credible to teachers
whom they have to advise.

How does it help your career prospects?

If you fit the bill and are confident in dealing with a wide range of
age groups, and you are competent in communicating with adults,
this is a handy escalator to the top. After a few years, many of them
go straight on to deputy headships. Others enjoy the job so much

they choose to stay in it while others go on to become advisors and inspectors.

If you intend using it as a jumping-off step to deputy headship, getting the timing right is crucial. For a primary teacher, it is wise only to be an advisory teacher for four or five years at the most. After that, you can become so out of touch with other subjects that you tend to feel de-skilled and it's difficult to adjust to the wide curriculum of the primary classroom. This is not such a difficult adjustment for a secondary teacher as they only have to teach two, or at the most, three subjects.

The advantages

- Some advisory teachers say it's less pressure than being a class/subject teacher with class/es of 30 all day, every day.
- You don't have that day-to-day accountability which causes such stress to teachers.
- You have greater control of how you organize your day. You are not straitjacketed by a timetable.
- You can concentrate on one subject, usually the subject which interests you most, and so become an expert at it.
- You can escape from being stuck in the same classroom/s every day and you don't have the tedious task of marking piles of books.
- You escape from the tedious nitty-gritty tasks like nagging pupils to keep the classroom tidy, filing masses of pupils' work, putting up displays and sticking labels on everything.
- If the class you're teaching is horrendous, you have the pleasure of seeing them off after the lesson, happy in the knowledge that you might never see them again, or for at least a year or two.
- Variety is the spice of life. Every week is different, so if you're a secondary teacher, you never have the thought of teaching the same tired-out class last thing on Friday afternoon hanging over you like a Sword of Damocles all week.
- It is a highly privileged job because you're in a position to see lots of different teachers working and so you pick up lots of ideas and acquire a wealth of knowledge and skills.
- You have time to read and research to extend your own

knowledge and understanding; and the opportunity to share it with other teachers gives great satisfaction.

- You have more time to reflect on and study issues around the job.
- You have more opportunity for training for future professional development than other teachers. You don't have to fight for time off to go on courses and conferences.

The disadvantages

- Less financial stability. Sometimes they have fixed-term contracts. The feeling of insecurity is uncomfortable.
- Less job satisfaction because you are never with the same class for long so you can't compare the pupils' work at the beginning and end of the year and see the improvement.
- Building relationships is more difficult because you have to work in a new set of schools every week with a large and wide ranging number of teachers. When you meet them in the Teachers' Centre, you can usually remember their faces but not always their names and in which school you have met them.
- You have more 'loose ends' than teachers based in one school, because your work is spread out in so many places. It is more difficult to make keep all the plates spinning.
- If you spend a week working in lots of different environments there can be a feeling of being detached.
- The holidays are shorter: you have administrative work to do when the schools are closed. You still have to take holidays at peak times.

Tips from experienced advisory teachers

Before you start

Some say that there's not much clear induction into the job, partly because there may not be a line manager who has done the job him/herself. You have got to be proactive in approaching line managers and more experienced advisory teachers for guidance as to which groups of people you should be working with and the best way to establish contact.

Others emphasize that it's important to speak to teachers with confidence and enthusiasm. They will only want to listen to your message if it sounds as if you are certain of your facts and it will improve the quality of their teaching.

Delivering single lessons to be observed by teachers

Preparation
Some advisory teachers advise new colleagues to start small and find their feet before trying anything too adventurous and until they're used to the job.

Before every lesson it's essential to talk to the class teacher to set:

- The pitch. Find out about their previous work to set the lesson as near the right level as possible.
- The objective. Always negotiate with the class teacher, making sure it's clear to you both and try to make sure you stay on track with it.
- Feasibility. Don't try to be all things to all teachers. If you can't deliver what the class teacher wants, say so.

Delivering lessons
- Make quality the key word. It's tempting to pack loads into each lesson, but you'll impress more by doing less, well.
- Since every class is new, spend three or four minutes at the beginning of the lesson having fun or telling a joke and being Mr/Ms nice guy, to warm them up and get them on your side.

When you've finished
- At the end of the lesson mentally evaluate whether the outcome is what you intended. Give out evaluation forms and compare your assessment with the teachers. Some teachers can't be bothered filling them in, while others may be only too eager to do so if they have 'suggestions for improvement'. If they don't fill them in you can safely take that as a sign they're satisfied.
- You can also evaluate your success by watching the reaction of the staff next time you enter the school. That should let you know if they think you're worth listening to.

Planning and delivering a scheme of partnership lessons

You can be invited into a school to assist teachers in preparing and teaching a set of lessons in order to develop their skill in an area of the curriculum. This is much more satisfying because you start to build up a relationship with a class and see some progress.

Some teachers ask for assistance and so make you welcome, but others feel pressured by your presence, particularly if the head has invited you in because they are functioning below par. It is important to make the teacher feel at ease and emphasize that you are there to support only. Teachers often relax when they find the advisory teacher is actually giving practical help to make their job easier.

Preparation and delivering lessons

- Before working in partnership, lay down the ground rules with the class teacher. Ask what discipline strategies are used, what they allow and encourage and what they don't. Who is delivering each part of each lesson? Does the class teacher mind if you chip in to her lesson with extra information? Who decides if pupils can go to the loo and who marks the work afterwards?
- If you can, spend a lesson observing the class with whom you'll be working.
- Spend a lot of time listening to the class/subject teachers. Ask what is working well in their classrooms.
- Make sure the teacher gives you tightly drawn up objectives about what they want to achieve. It doesn't matter if you have to modify them as time goes on, provided of course that the class/subject teacher agrees.
- When planning the lessons, ask if any other adult – support teacher, classroom assistant, parent volunteer – will be in the classroom. It is worth involving them. Make sure you're introduced to them and learn their names and make sure they have a specific role to play in the lesson.
- Watch other teachers closely. You can always pick up ideas to use and pass on. It's not cheating: most teachers are delighted when the advisory teacher asks to use their ideas.

When you have finished the sequence of lessons
- At the end, evaluate with the class teacher how well the outcome matched the original objective. Discuss it with the teacher.
- Try to make sure that whatever new practices the teacher has learnt are disseminated into the rest of the school. This probably means asking the head for an Inset period with the objective of spreading the expertise. It also means liaising with the curriculum postholder to have the practice documented in the school policy.
- Before you leave, always thank them for their cooperation and say what you have enjoyed/learnt from the experience. Keep the atmosphere friendly, by making them see it has been a two-way benefit as you may need to go back there.

Delivering lectures to teachers
This usually happens after school or on the Inset days before the start of term.

- If visiting a school, start by saying something positive about it – its friendly atmosphere, the attractive display work, recent Ofsted/examination success.
- Make at least part of the session practical. Teachers usually prefer it to sitting listening.
- When addressing a whole staffroom, try to address individually as many teachers as you can, all if possible. If there's a coffee break try to circulate and chat to people.
- Always make sure you give your teachers something which they can take away and actually use. Otherwise they feel they have wasted their time.
- Give the teachers a typed précis of the main points of the topic. They can enjoy the activity better if they don't have to make notes during it.
- On the rare occasion that you might be faced with a hostile or rude group of staff, at all costs keep your cool and let them see you're in control. When the session is over tell the head politely but firmly you have better things to do with your time, and will not be returning unless you receive an apology.

Practical everyday issues

- Keep a diary of notes of what you have done in each session. If you have planned different things in six different schools, it could be embarrassing if you mixed them up.
- In the boot of your car carry the documentation for your subject and handouts of ideas and information on what's new in your subject. Teachers are always pleased if you can produce it quickly.
- Before you pass on lots of extra paper to read, ask teachers if they want it, so you don't have the uncomfortable situation of teachers taking, out of politeness, stuff they haven't time to read and then throwing it into the bin.
- Keep a list of websites handy for teachers to refer to for more ideas.
- Always carry a little bag of teabags, a mug and a spoon because in some schools everybody has their own tea and coffee and you feel uncomfortable scrounging.
- If they offer you tea or coffee always ask if the have a tin for visitors to pay. Most schools are hospitable but a few are fussy about details like this.
- Don't forget to fill in your mileage claim as you go along because if you leave it to the end of the month, you will have forgotten the details.

Keeping an eye on the future

- Don't forget the filing cabinet. Keep a record of every lesson, and keep every Inset lecture filed according to age group or topic. It's bound to be reusable.
- After a few years, think about your next move. This is an effective jumping-off post to be a deputy head or advisor. Being in different schools puts you in the advantageous position where you can see them from the inside and get to know their staff before you apply to them.

14 One step up to be an advisor

What is an advisor?

Advisors are highly skilled and experienced teachers who are employed to coordinate and inspect the quality of teaching in one or more areas of the curriculum. They are also responsible for introducing changes in government and LEA policy into the schools. They are not attached to any one school and are normally based at the LEA offices. Every LEA employs a team of advisors to ensure that the best quality of education is delivered to their pupils at both primary and secondary level. They work closely with other advisors, inspectors and headteachers.

What does an advisor do?

The job has a wide variety of responsibilities which are outlined below. Obviously no one has to cope with all of them at once. An advisor has to:

- do the Ofsted training and carry out inspections;
- go into schools in their own authority to help them prepare for their Ofsted inspections;
- ensure that one subject, for example maths, is taught effectively in every age group throughout the LEA;
- oversee other aspects of school life, such as behaviour management and attendance;
- run training programmes for classroom assistants at the Teachers' Centre;
- run family literacy and numeracy programmes in schools;
- makes sure that changes in teaching format, for example literacy hour, are put into practice in schools within the LEA;

- run courses for teachers to introduce changes in teaching methods;
- support heads and teachers in bringing about school improvement by running school-based training during Inset days and whole-staff meetings;
- work with teachers in their classroom to help them improve;
- monitor schools to ensure they carry out LEA policy;
- monitor schools' progress in improving.

Salary and pensions

Their posts are normally permanent and they are often paid on the Soulbury salary scale at a much higher point than advisory teachers. A new advisor can expect a rise of four or five thousand. They may pay pension contributions into the Local Government Pensions scheme or the Teachers' Superannuation Scheme. This however can vary from one LEA to the next and needs to be checked out before you apply.

Advantages

An advisor's job carries many of the same advantages as an advisory teacher's job, but it has the added perk that you have the power to carry your vision through and make changes happen. This makes it a tremendously satisfying job. Advisors enjoy much higher salary and status than advisory teachers or advanced skills teachers.

Disadvantages

- In recent years governments have taken a progressively greater role in LEA policy and so there's less freedom in how one carries out the job.
- If you work in a difficult LEA, you are monitored more closely and there is much more pressure on you from central government to work to their agenda.
- In some LEAs the number of advisors has diminished and a smaller group of people are expected to cover the same work. This adds to the pressure.

From the outside looking in, this might look like a suitable job for a teacher who is eager to escape from the classroom, but that is a misconception. In order to cope with it you have to be a highly competent teacher, able to give a range of ideas to teachers and demonstrate your teaching prowess confidently.

So what skills do advisors need?

All of the points below apply to both primary and secondary teachers.

- High competency across the full age range because you may need to deliver Inset from early years to A-level.
- High academic ability to absorb texts quickly and put theory into practice effectively. Anyone finding difficulty with coping in a classroom would not be a suitable candidate.
- Vision to transform the script on the page into workable practice which teachers will find effective. Where they judge that the teachers will not readily accept the details outlined in the government document they must adapt it to make it practical for them.
- Inter-personal skills are an absolute necessity. Like an advisory teacher they need to have a comfortable working relationship with a wide range of teachers, heads and inspectors.
- Sound judgement. Being an advisor is an even more challenging job than being an advisory teacher because one has to be far more judgmental. It looks easy, just sitting at the back of the class watching someone else doing the work while all you have to do is the criticizing. Of course, one has to make sure the criticisms follow the Ofsted criteria and one has to produce evidence to back up your comments. The responsibility of making judgements about teachers' teaching is huge because you owe it to the teachers to make absolutely certain your judgements are accurate and fair.
- Multi-tasking skills. Advisors have a huge brief, for example, they have to have an overview of how a subject is taught in every school in the LEA from Nursery up to A-level. They have to keep up with the changes and always be seen to be on the ball with the latest documents about government and LEA policy. Mentally, it's a very exacting job.

Advice from the experienced advisors

Starting off

- During your first half-term on the job, try to visit as many of the schools in the LEA as you can. There can be a tremendous difference in schools in one area to another. It is important to have an overview of the geography of each school, its atmosphere and the cultural and ethnic mix of each.
- Make yourself acquainted with as many heads, deputies and teachers as you can manage and make sure they know you and what your role is.

Maintain your credibility

- Get into classrooms as much as you can. It's too easy to find yourself spending too many hours in front of a computer screen. Also, advisors sometimes have the image of being out of touch by spending their time in the office talking to heads.
- Make sure you're closely acquainted with the National Curriculum and all the government documents for your subject because your role is to implement the national strategies and LEA policy effectively within schools.

Putting policy into practice

- It is tempting to believe that your sole purpose is to deliver every government initiative and strategy. It is important to respect the professionalism of teachers, and acknowledge the difference in the tasks facing those in widely different areas. You must be willing to modify government strategies to suit individual schools.
- Teachers are disenchanted with governments constantly introducing new initiatives and strategies. An advisor must be creative enough to make them attractive and interesting for teachers to want to take them on board. It's a bit like a teacher trying to make each lesson interesting for reluctant pupils.
- Make sure you have clear in your mind what you're aiming for in developing your subject creatively within the LEA.
- Talk with other advisors about any school must be confidential.
- There is a danger in always trying to please the hierarchy. It is

important to do your networking downwards to the heads and teachers, as your ultimate aim is to support teachers and pupils, not pander to the political agenda of the LEAs and government.

Inspections

- Try to only carry out Ofsted inspections alongside your own colleagues whom you know and trust.
- Try to avoid doing Ofsted inspections in other LEAs. To do the job properly you have to spend a week preparing, a week doing it and another week writing it up. This takes you away from your own job, where you want to be spending your time helping your own schools.
- Have it clear in your mind at all times that if a school is not coping, the whole focus of your task is to guide and improve it, not to destroy it.

For the confident, experienced teacher with an inventive mind, personal skills and a voracious appetite for reading, this is a challenging and satisfying post. The advisors to whom I spoke clearly enjoyed the work and gained great job satisfaction.

15 Could you be an advanced skills teacher?

What is an advanced skills teacher (AST)?

AST status is high among teachers. They are teachers who have demonstrated excellence in almost every area of their job and been assessed and awarded AST status. After being thoroughly inspected and their performance assessed and awarded AST status, they continue in the same post in their school, but are released from it one day per week to go to other schools to carry out their role of supporting the professional development of other teachers.

Salary and pensions

ASTs have a different pay scale to other teachers and at the time of writing (2004) the AST scale has 27 points and starts at a figure which is about £3,400 higher than point M6 on the main professional scale. ASTs also enjoy higher status than ordinary class/subject teachers. Their jobs are permanent and they pay into the same teachers' pension scheme as other teachers.

How do you get AST status?

This position is reached after teachers have applied to be assessed for it, and they've been formally notified that their application is accepted; and they've been formally assessed and inspected satisfactorily. This process can take up to several months.

What is an AST asked to do?

- Inreach work. Helping teachers in their own school to improve.
- Outreach work. Helping teachers in other schools to improve.

Even if an AST has particular skills in a few subjects, they will be expected to take on assignments right across the board. Whether in your own or another school, you will undertake projects to help teachers to develop better strategies for:

- planning schemes of lessons;
- preparing resources;
- making lessons fun;
- behaviour management;
- writing school policies;
- organizing the curriculum for their post or year group;
- preparing model lessons for Ofsted;
- helping teachers achieve targets set out for them after Ofsted – this can be done through shared planning, delivering parts of the lessons for teachers to observe, team teaching and giving feedback;
- the monitoring process.

Apart from individual subjects, there are ASTs to give support

- in the mentoring process;
- to middle management;
- to classroom assistants.

Why be an AST?

Teachers follow this route because they love the interaction of the classroom and enjoy helping other teachers to improve. They are ambitious and want to progress but do not want to go down the deputy head/head route because these jobs take them out of the classroom and into the office. An AST post is a very creative job, and those I have interviewed clearly derive a lot of job pleasure from it. To me the post of AST sounds enjoyable because you spend about 20 per cent of each week working with adults who appreciate your effort.

What qualities do you need to be an AST?

As well as being all-round excellent teachers, all the ASTs I have met possess the following qualities:

- high level of commitment to the profession;
- highly developed interpersonal skills;
- positive attitudes towards helping other teachers to improve;
- an ability to find opportunities to be involved in other people's professional development;
- ability to take pride in the achievements of other teachers.

So where does it lead?

ASTs are well placed to becoming AST coordinators, deputy heads, heads, advisors or inspectors, though many of them prefer the creative satisfaction of their work in the classroom.

Applying for AST status

Becoming an AST is a bit like the promised land – terrific when you arrive, as long as the journey doesn't wipe you out before you reach it.

The process of becoming an AST is designed for the pleasure of paperholics, and is not for the faint-hearted. Before applying to be an AST, a teacher must have had at least three years of experience and had a high record of success in almost every area of the job. Most applicants have had much more than three years.

They have to fill in a detailed booklet of questions in which they aim to demonstrate standards of excellence, supported by a substantial amount of evidence. If you hope to be an AST, it's important to collect evidence from early on in your teaching career. It is worth allocating several files in your filing cabinet for the purpose.

The application form can be downloaded from www.teachernet. gov.uk.professional/ast.

The application form gives the criteria for fulfilling each of the categories. You must write a detailed statement to show that you qualify in the following areas.

1   Excellent results/outcomes.
2   Excellent subject and/or specialist knowledge.
3   Excellent ability to plan.
4   Excellent ability to teach, manage pupils and maintain discipline.

5   Excellent ability to assess and evaluate.
6   Excellent ability to advise and support other teachers.

You and your head must complete the form and send it to the address supplied, keeping a copy to remind you of the criteria for passing each section. If accepted you'll be allocated an assessor who will visit you in your school. You will then have about three months to prepare.

Several pieces of documentary evidence are required for each section and one must add details and evidence of continuing professional development. Failure to fulfil any one of the sections cannot be compensated by brilliance in another. It is necessary to collect evidence over a period of up to three years. It's a good idea to have a folder for each category's evidence.

What can you use as evidence?

Below is a list of items suggested by ASTs for fulfilling each category.

Excellent results/outcomes
- Comments from the assessment coordinator when monitoring your assessment file.
- Written feedback from senior members of staff who have monitored your lessons.
- Registers of special educational needs, ethnic minority achievement or more able pupils. Photocopy the relevant pages and highlight those pupils for whose improvement you can claim some credit.
- Letters of thanks from parents and pupils.
- SATs, QCA, GCSE, AS-level and A-level results from the previous three years.
- Records of tracking of individual pupils over three years or more.
- Before and after examples of pupils' work over a year.
- Copies of pupils' targets and the outcomes.

Excellent subject and/or specialist knowledge
- Certificates or diplomas you possess in your subjects.
- Certificate of recognition if you have been designated as a teacher of excellence in any subject.

- New Opportunities Funding certificate for basic computer skills.
- Ofsted report – copy any pages which refer specifically to you and highlight them.
- Your Ofsted grades.
- Insets you have attended.
- Details of Insets you have delivered to the staff – outline of the content, overhead projector sheets and evaluation sheets.
- Feedback notes from people who have monitored your lessons.

Excellent ability to plan

- Plans for your subject of responsibility: the overview of all the topics to be studied in your subject from Reception to Year 6, or Year 7 to Year 13; medium-term and weekly plans for as much of the last three years as you've got; and the written feedback from the senior staff who monitored them.
- Examples of literacy and numeracy hour planning (primary), medium-term and weekly plans (secondary) and written feedback.
- Example of notes you've given to NQTs or Graduate Teacher Programme students, classroom assistants or bilingual teaching assistants for whom you're a mentor.
- Plans for booster classes.
- Revision plans for SATs, QCAs, GCSE, AS-levels and A-levels.
- Contributions you've made to the staff development plan.
- Notes you've made for staff prior to events like sports day, Ofsted, pupils' parties, parents' evenings, pupils' productions, end of term finishing off and preparations for new term.
- Letters of thanks from students whom you've helped during your teaching practice

Excellent ability to teach, manage pupils and maintain discipline

- Ofsted lesson feedback.
- Ofsted commendation.
- Feedback notes from senior members of staff who have monitored your lessons.

- Examples of work produced by pupils during your lessons, especially extra work which pupils have done voluntarily.
- Written details of your behaviour strategies.
- Extracts from your behaviour file.
- Photographs of pupils doing something exciting in class, on school journeys, day trips and extra-curricular activities, and parents helping in class.
- A written statement of your view on the hidden curriculum.
- Threshold application file.

Excellent ability to assess and evaluate
- Assessment coordinator feedback.
- Evaluations of own lessons carried out for planning further years.
- Evaluations which you have written on lessons you've observed.
- Copies of pupils' work which you have marked and evaluated, for example for report writing or tracking pupils' progress.

Excellent ability to advise and support other teachers
- Monitoring and observation forms you have given to other teachers.
- Details of work you have carried out to link the Ofsted report to the school development plan.
- Details of all the Inset you have delivered to the staff, including overhead projector acetates, PowerPoint presentations you've constructed and handouts prepared for the staff.
- Reference you have written for a colleague.
- Any letters of thanks you've received from parents, governors, colleagues or heads.
- Induction advice to guide NQTs, student teachers, classroom assistants, parent helpers and community service students.
- Revision plans for SATs, QCAs, GCSEs, AS-levels and A-levels.
- Health and safety plans.
- Lists of useful websites you have delivered to the staff.

The last of these six sections is the most difficult because teachers may not have had much opportunity to support other teachers before becoming an AST. You also have to show that you can be effective in schools other than your own, although you have not yet had the opportunity to go into other schools to advise and support other teachers. To get over this hurdle you can offer to give demonstration lessons in other people's classes in your non-contact periods. Some suggest contacting the advisory teacher for your subject and offering to be involved in In-service training in the local Teachers' Centre.

Continuing professional development

- School policies you've updated.
- Schemes of work you've written.
- School magazine/newsletter to which you have contributed.
- Photographs of school production, netball/football teams and choir/dance teams with which you've been involved.
- First-aid/ NOF certificate.
- Notes from performance management interviews.
- Notes from observation, monitoring and evaluation of your subject specialism.

Obviously, some of the evidence can fit into more than one section. It's time consuming and tedious to put all this together and it can only be done if you have kept all your paperwork for a few years.

Preparing for the day of assessment

There is plenty of help available.

- There are courses to help you put the folder together. ASTs go through the standards and show candidates the relevant information.
- Contact the AST coordinator in your LEA and ask him/her to meet you and your head to explain the finer details of what the assessor will be looking for and to offer advice.
- Contact recently appointed ASTs who can show you how to set out your evidence in a professional manner. Some suggest cutting and sticking your comments from each section of the application form at the front of each section with an index and numbering each page for easy access. Some ASTs may allow you to look at their folders to see how to set it out and the types of evidence you can use.

Assessment day

The assessor arrives around 8am and spends the day in your school examining you. S/he interviews you and examines your file of evidence in detail. Teachers are frequently nervous and this sometimes reduces their performance but remember that most aspiring ASTs pass this examination.

S/he then observes you teaching two lessons. It is not enough to do ordinary run-of-the-mill lessons: it has to be of superior quality, have something extra to show that you're an excellent teacher. ASTs tell me it is worse than Ofsted because you're the only one in the school being assessed and everyone will know if you fail.

The assessor then interviews the headteacher. You cannot succeed without your head's agreement, but a head would not let the procedure go this far unless s/he intended to support you.

The assessor then makes a draft report of 400 words. At the end of the day you're called in to hear the report and be told your fate.

If not successful, don't worry. Just ask for feedback as to which category you did not meet and think of it as a useful experience to help you to re-apply in the future. This is a very high hurdle and there is no disgrace in missing it on the first attempt.

Acquiring the status is an immensely elating experience because you are being hailed as an excellent teacher by members of the upper echelons of the profession, though rather daunting when you realize you have an image and expectations to live up to.

The advantages of the job

- Job satisfaction. One AST told me of her delight when a couple of NQTs who were on target to fail, improved and went on to be successful with support from herself. Another told me how she was thrilled when a teacher observed her methods of control, adopted them and saw immediate improvement in the pupil's behaviour.
- It is such an achievement to obtain AST status that you will automatically be shortlisted and probably appointed to any post for which you apply.
- The long-winded process won't seem so bad when you realize that you will no longer have to bother reapplying for movement on the upper pay spine every couple of years.

- During your 20 per cent release from the classroom you can be completely autonomous and organize yourself to do the job in your own way.
- Some say that the day in another school is an absolute pleasure because the pupils enjoy having another adult to help; you're delivering a lesson with a creative element, which they enjoy; and you are focusing on helping the teacher and so the task is less stressful.
- It is a privilege to go into other schools and pick up new ideas and improve your own skills. Even ASTs are still learning.
- Some LEAs provide their ASTs with a laptop computer and digital camera.
- The extra £3,000+ comes in handy when you're doing your shopping.

What the experienced ASTs advise

- Ease yourself in gently. Many new ASTs take up their post brimming over with enthusiasm and determination to lift everyone up to their very high standards. It is tempting to take on lots of commitments, but most ASTs say don't take on too much to start with. If you spread your butter too thinly, no one gets the benefit of it.
- Initially it's hard to keep both your own class achieving and the professional support for others moving at the same time. Most ASTs say persevere and this becomes easier with practice.
- When you start it's best to use your 20 per cent timetable to benefit your own school. This gives you practice, before you start working in unfamiliar territory.
- At the end of each day out of your own class, always give feedback to the headteacher on what you've done and achieved. They appreciate being kept informed and it lets them see you're not wasting time.

Keep your path smooth
- If the teacher who covers your class during your release time cannot cope, you might start to dread returning to an untidy classroom or being given a list of the previous day's problems

to sort out before you start. One AST solved the problem by using a few sessions to induct the teacher covering her own class.

- It is important to impress on the head, in the interests of the pupils, the importance of employing teachers who are flexible enough to adapt to classes to be covered.

Protect your 20 per cent

- Some heads try to cut the release time of their AST staff down to less than 20 per cent. This means you have to teach first, then travel to the next school and this cuts your time down even further. If your school is understaffed and really needs you, it can be difficult to get out of doing it. If so, try to compromise with something like, 'All right for the meantime, but I should like to have my full 20 per cent entitlement as soon you can manage it'.
- Some heads try to use you as a supply to cover classes of absent colleagues. If this happens it's best to be strong and politely but firmly say, 'Sorry, I can't, I'm doing something else'. If it proves to be a regular problem it's best to organize work away from your own school premises completely.

Outreach work – in other schools

In some LEAs, ASTs find projects in other schools through the AST coordinator who receives requests from headteachers. In others, teachers find their own assignments by approaching schools. The latter gives ASTs greater flexibility to carry out the assignments which interest them most.

What the ASTs advise

- Before you start in another school, make sure you talk to the head and get specific targets of what s/he wants you to achieve.
- Try to make sure you organize your own timetable for the day.
- Keep a log of what you do in each part of the day, give feedback to the teacher and a copy to the head, and perhaps the AST coordinator if s/he needs it.
- In the outreach school it's more beneficial to plan the lessons in partnership, usually with the AST introducing it and the

class teacher taking over. This builds up a teacher's confidence more than your taking the whole lesson with the class teacher merely observing; or the class teacher taking the lesson and you observing and giving feedback.

- Communication becomes problematical when you are not on-site. Planning lessons on the telephone, fax and email is not effective, so it's best to plan the following week's work with the teacher before you leave each day. The personal touch always works best.

- Make notes of your share of the work and the resources you have to provide, because it soon gets buried under your own work when you return to your own class.

- Also ask the heads in the outreach schools to designate a time at the end of the day when you can give feedback. You may have to be assertive about pinning the head down to a time because they are always so busy.

- Great tact is needed. Sometimes you'll be invited to a school by a head to support much older and more experienced teachers. This can cause resentment if teachers think they are being taught to suck eggs. Smile and start by saying something positive about the work they've already done. If they've done something special, say it's a great idea and ask if you can use it elsewhere.

- ASTs have their own specialisms but are not always asked to give support in these areas. This can be frustrating in the beginning, but if you accept any offer to get started, you can then mention to the head as you finish the type of project you're looking for. When you establish a reputation for skill in any one area, it is easier to get assignments.

Support for the AST

- Difficulties arise if there's a conflict of ideals between the head and the AST. Finding a tactful and professional way of not compromising your principles can be an ordeal. If all else fails, you can ask your AST mentor for support.

- If an AST has any other problems which they cannot solve on their own, they can also refer them to their mentor.

Don't forget your own career

While supporting others, remember to look after yourself. Make a wish–list of the things you want to do to help yourself. Use some of your days out of class to make resources or visit other schools which are successful in areas where you wish to improve.

Of all the teachers I interviewed, ASTs were among the most content with their job.

16 How to survive Ofsted

Ofsted and proposed changes

Prior to 1990 general inspections in schools were rare and I knew teachers who worked for decades without having to suffer one. Those happy days are long gone and at the time of writing, the Department's Office for Standards in Education, commonly known as Ofsted and a few other things, visits all state schools in Britain about once every four to six years for a thorough inspection.

At this point in time (2004), the Ofsted experience requires much preparation and generates widely varying amounts of stress, depending on the school.

In February 2004 Ofsted published a consultation document proposing shorter and more frequent inspections at shorter notice. Three-quarters of their respondents welcomed the suggestion, though many wanted a longer period of notice than the two to five days suggested.

Full details can be found on www.ofsted.gov.uk/ofstednews. At the time of writing, Ofsted's proposals include:

1 Inspections at least every three years.
2 Inspections which are short but rigorous.
3 Giving two to five days' notice.

Pilots for the new format will continue throughout 2004–05 and if approved by parliament the new format could be in place by September 2005. If the above period of notice, or similar, is adopted, the period of feverish pre-Ofsted activity will disappear, although it might be replaced by a few weeks or months of nervous uncertainty when the time is nigh. At the moment, it's impossible to forecast the exact timings and formats of Ofsted inspections because they're as yet undecided.

Whatever the outcome of the pilot studies, when you arrive in a school for a preliminary visit, it would still be wise to find out discreetly when the last Ofsted inspection was, and add on the appropriate number of years to estimate the occasion of the next one. You can also find it on www.ofsted.gov.uk. It's well worthwhile, probably essential, to read their last Ofsted report on the website. If a visit from Ofsted is imminent, say within your first two terms, you might like to take that into consideration before making up your mind whether to apply for the job. If you like the school, the prospect may not deter you because, as a new arrival, you cannot be blamed for any problems as long as your lessons are prepared and delivered satisfactorily. If the school is very problematical it may be advisable to try elsewhere.

Once you're established in a school, when the time is nigh, visit www.ofsted.gov.uk because I've known inspections to be on the website before the dreaded brown envelope hits the school doormat. In the past, teachers who found inspections stressful sometimes had enough time to find another job and escape. If the notice period is cut to a few days, you cannot possibly do so: your only course is to keep all your paperwork up to date and in place until it's over.

The announcement

So far I've survived four general inspections, two of which were by Ofsted. While it's always a stressful experience for everyone I believe it's worst for the head, who has to take ultimate responsibility for everyone else's foibles, as well as his/her own.

Generally, you can expect the head to walk into the staff meeting, even more grim-faced than usual, clutching an untidy pile of educational magazines, catalogues and letters close to his/her chest – a sign that some unpalatable news is about to be delivered. S/he takes up the usual seat in front of the messy coffee table, littered with unwashed coffee mugs, foul-smelling ashtrays, unread circulars and copies of *The Teacher* and *The Professional Teacher*, vying with each other for the more prominent position.

When the bombshell finally drops that HM's Government intends sending some representatives to give the staff the benefit of their judgement, subdued, silent gloom descends and each can see the others' shoulders droop and jaws drop open.

The staffroom cynic usually makes a disgusted remark like, 'Well I couldn't care less what they think! If they think they can do a better job, within the constraints in which we work, they can get in the bloody classroom and show us'.

Another giggles and says 'Oh God, I suppose the school's consumption of valium is about to shoot up'. Occasionally someone's face turns white and their jaw starts shaking as they gasp for air.

Someone might say, sanctimoniously, 'Be strong, everyone, be ready to stand up to them. Ofsted's nothing'. I even had a colleague once who said she liked Ofsted because it made everyone do everything properly! Beware of the last type. They depress you more, the longer the Sword of Damocles wait goes on.

In the past, Ofsted inspectors had a bad name. A tragic case where a teacher committed suicide after negative feedback from an inspector, not to mention some well-aimed complaints from heads, have perhaps resulted in a softening of their tone in recent years. I know of one head who telephoned Ofsted during an inspection and named an inspector whom he did not want to entertain again because he had reduced so many women teachers to tears!

The pre-Ofsted visit

At present, before the inspection, the registered inspector visits the school for a day to become familiar with it and the head. Some are pleasant and friendly, discreetly pointing out to the head things to put right before the inspection. Some are fairly businesslike, giving nothing away. At the end of the day the inspector addresses the whole staff to give an outline of how the inspection will take its course, i.e. how many observed lessons each might have, who might be interviewed, what they're looking for and what paperwork they want ready.

They usually give a polished performance, sometimes reassuring the staff that they know how they feel as they themselves have been inspected as class teachers and as heads themselves. They then add some reassurance that if a lesson goes wrong, it will not be classified as unsatisfactory as long as the teacher manages to pull it back on track. They often add that serious misbehaviour by pupils will not be held against the school as long as it's dealt with effectively. In fact, effective handling is seen as a definite point in the school's favour.

They then tell the staff that there are several grades: excellent, very good, good, satisfactory, unsatisfactory and poor.

However if the notice period is cut to days, this episode might be cut out completely.

The stress factor

Heads, understandably, usually become rigorous in their task of checking every detail of the school's procedures during this period. Coupled with the private knowledge of their own failure, they could face terrible humiliation at the Board of Governors' meetings, and would have to attend headteachers' meetings where most of their colleagues have passed their inspection. They may even lose their job and they've a mortgage to pay like everyone else.

Although some chalk-face teachers disagree, I still believe that the head's job is the most stressful during the Ofsted period because they'll have to accept responsibility if the school fails, and unlike the teachers, they would find it almost impossible to find another job with the same salary. It is not surprising that some heads, wittingly or otherwise, subject their staff to so much stress that tears and arguments over trivial issues are too common a feature of the staffroom in the weeks leading up to, and during, the inspection. The obvious benefit of a shorter notice period would be to cut out this stressful period.

Whether it's a long a or short notice period, this will be an anxious time for you, so try not to react against the head being over critical or seeming less kindly or grateful than usual. S/he is human like the rest of us. It is also wise not to spend too much time near those teachers who are anxious or depressed at the prospect, unless of course, you are confident enough to reassure them or cheer them up.

Even the most capable teachers can become anxious. A friend who is a head once told me that during Ofsted the quality of education in his school always goes down because his excellent, hardworking staff are so nervous they never perform at their optimal level.

What steps can everyone take to relieve stress?

Minimizing stress is a whole-school responsibility and the key word is 'teamwork'. The united effort of the staff is much greater than the sum of each person's individual contribution, if every adult is there to support everyone else, not look out for themselves.

This includes the auxiliary staff. Make the classroom assistants, welfare assistants and secretaries feel included and you'll be fostering a sense of pride and increasing the support they give you. If they're pulling their weight and taking pride in their work, make sure they know you appreciate it. When the inspection is over make sure you pass on to your classroom assistants any positive feedback which the inspectors have made which applies to them. Every little bit helps to provide a happier atmosphere and reduce stress levels.

Countdown to the day

This will vary according to the length of the notice period.

The head asks everyone to change all the display boards to make them look especially attractive. You can't avoid it, so try an answer, like, 'Yes, lovely idea, but can you please confirm that after the inspection, they need not be changed for another two terms/the remainder of the school year?' (whichever is the longer). S/he'll probably be so stressed out s/he's bound to agree and you won't find it such a waste of time if you know your effort will have a longer-lasting benefit. If the notice period is short they will probably only ask for the more jaded display boards to be changed.

Before an inspection, heads and senior staff sometimes walk around teachers' classrooms and tell them what to remove, add and tidy up, examine their planning folders, check that the pupils' books are all marked and generally seem very critical. It feels like an invasion of your space and it's irritating but try not to let it annoy you. It's not personal and they are under stress too.

If the countdown period is cut to a few days you will probably try to anticipate the date, counting on whatever number of years they decide on since the last inspection and having your room looking attractive, just in case . . .

Where the parents come in

Ofsted takes the views of parents seriously and so it's quite likely that they will continue to canvass their opinions even if the timing and format of the inspection is changed.

At the time of writing, before the inspection parents are given a form to fill in stating their views on the school's competence in delivering the curriculum, handling problems and providing lessons which are interesting and in a happy atmosphere. They are then invited to attend a meeting with the inspectors to give their opinions on how effective the school is.

Parents are notoriously negligent at returning these forms and a small number returned is seen as a sign that the school has poor parent/teacher communication or does not involve the parents enough. It is wise to photocopy spares and if parents have not returned their forms, try to anticipate whether they would give a positive or negative view of the school. Obviously you need only chase up the former category.

You should always read the reply forms, to prepare a defence to any negative criticism. It is tempting to destroy any which have very destructive remarks but not worth the risk, because those are the parents who will most probably turn up at the meeting and collar the inspector to elaborate on their comments. Being caught out destroying the evidence against you would grease the slope to failure.

Members of staff are barred from attending the evening meeting unless their children attend the school. Parents often don't bother attending the pre-Ofsted meeting with the inspectors. Teachers should always chase up those parents whom they know are satisfied with the school and gently persuade them to attend. I always used the line, 'If parents don't turn up, they'll say we're not involving them enough and hold it against us,' and put on a worried expression.

The staff members whose children attend the school should always attend this meeting, firstly to praise the school's efforts in providing for their pupils, and secondly to relate back to the head and staff everything said about them. As with the forms, if they know what has been said, it gives everyone a chance to prepare their defence.

Heads of department and teachers with posts of responsibility

This can be a testing and stressful period for these teachers because they must take responsibility for the overall running of their departments and therefore the quality of other teachers' lessons. However, they can also take pressure off the shoulders of their more junior colleagues.

- In secondary schools, it's a sensible idea to provide each teacher in your department with a paper wallet and blank lesson plans to fill in for each lesson. Although it's extra work for you, go through them with a fine tooth comb and make any suggestions for improvement. If you do that properly, your seal of approval will give your junior colleagues confidence.

- In a primary school, Key Stage 1 coordinators should do likewise. Similarly postholders with responsibility for their subject. In a primary school it ends up with lots of people checking each others plans, but the mutual support and reassurance that evolves gives people confidence.

- In both primary and secondary schools, all postholders and departmental heads should tell their staff not to bother producing any plans for a week or two before, and the fortnight after, the inspection so they can concentrate on getting it perfect for the Ofsted week, and to reduce the stress generated by the glut of paperwork in the last two points.

- Dig up the school policy for teaching your subject of responsibility and draw up a list of questions which you expect the inspectors to ask about how your subject is taught. Add the answers which you think appropriate and distribute a copy to all of the staff in your department (secondary) or class teachers (primary).

- If necessary have a short meeting, no longer than 15 minutes, to clarify any points. Encourage other subject postholders to do the same. Teachers are often nervous about their interview with the inspectors and having a list of questions and answers to study beforehand can give them confidence.

- In some schools the head assembles the staff at the end of the day to relate any positive feedback and express appreciation. Those few minutes of encouragement can be vital in keeping the staff going. If your head doesn't do it, heads of department (secondary), Key Stage 1 coordinators and senior staff (primary) can do it. Your staff will appreciate your taking the time.

Senior management

- Grab all the Ofsted envelopes and tear them up before discarding them and suggest to the head and secretary that they don't leave any Ofsted headed notepaper lying around. I know someone who acquired one of each, possibly from a waste-paper bin, and used them successfully to send a hoax letter to a head telling him, in the middle of A-levels, that Ofsted would be paying them an impromptu visit the same day. An early morning uproar broke out in the staffroom and was only quelled when a phone call to Ofsted put their minds at ease.
- If the period of notice is long enough, impress on the head the need for a child-free day, for example 'Inset day', just before Ofsted for the staff to be prepared to the back teeth. If the notice is drastically reduced this may become impossible.

Preparing the lessons

Before an inspection the school is always tarted up to give a favourable impression. This is quite right in my view, but it's still the quality and delivering of lessons upon which the teachers stand or fall.

Some people say that you should never prepare anything special for Ofsted: you should allow them to see the school as it normally is. I should ignore that. If the inspectors give plenty of notice, they expect the school to look superb and the teachers to perform at their absolute best. It is fairly accepted practice that you play to the gallery if there's an inspector in the room. I never believe the teachers who say they don't do so.

That means that you **do** prepare something special to impress. As far as possible, only prepare lessons on topics at which you're proficient. If you're preparing a lesson which may be difficult to carry out, you can practise it in the week before the inspection with a similar one, if a notice period of a few days does not prevent you from doing so.

If at any stage you think of a more impressive lesson than the one on the plan, don't be afraid to change. In fact it would be foolish not to.

Don't be afraid to take risks. Inspectors give high grades to the adventurous lessons. If you plan something exciting which you fear might go wrong, you can always have a contingency plan of an easier lesson ready in case it does not work. I have done that. Knowing that you can save the situation if it goes wrong, gives you the confidence to try for the higher grade.

What to tell the pupils

On the day before the inspection explain to the pupils that there'll be inspectors in school for a few days, checking that everyone is working well. If your pupils are young enough or naïve enough, you can give the impression it's they who are being inspected. Just say that at the end of the week, they'll be telling the head which classes are working and behaving properly. It's not wise to try this one with pupils who are mature enough to know better. It would make you look nervous and a bit weak.

If you have a minority of problematical pupils, tell the class that if they work hard and behave well for the inspection, there'll be a celebration day when it's all over. You need the head's permission, but as long as teachers are putting in the effort to make the inspection a success, they usually agree to anything. When the day comes round, you'll be so relieved it's over, you won't mind the extended playtimes, loud music, games in the classroom and boring videos, too much.

Getting through it

If it's too short notice to escape or you think that moving school might be more painful than the grilling, then try the following.

Good practice

- You will sleep better if you have all the preparation done well in advance. Make sure the following day is organized before you leave each evening.
- If you have a class who are likely to misbehave, instigate an incentive scheme a few weeks before the inspection. Put a grid chart on the wall, with names down the side and, on a daily basis, offer points for good behaviour and effort with their work. Provide a small, inexpensive prize, like a bar of nut-free chocolate, at the end of the week for each of the two or three pupils who score the most points. Some pupils

respond better to being let off a homework task as a reward. Of course you only let them off revision-type homework so that you don't leave gaps in their knowledge.

- In Ofsted week, triple the number of points which the class can earn.
- Tell the class that if everyone works and behaves well for the inspection, no one will have a homework task for a week after the inspection. This is not damaging their education, because everyone is too shattered to set and mark homework for at least a week after Ofsted anyway.
- Offer the class a trip to the local pizza restaurant for lunch after it's over, everyone paying for themselves, of course. If someone has let the class down during the inspection do not, under any circumstances, take them on the trip. It undermines your discipline for the future and antagonizes the pupils who have made the effort.

Bad practice

- Taking a sickie in Ofsted week is a terrible idea. Other teachers may have to cover your classes in the week when they feel least able to cope with extra work, or the head has to find a supply at the last minute. It is much better to risk a poor grade from an inspector than irritate your colleagues, who are unlikely to believe that you're actually ill. I once knew a senior member of staff who rang in to say he had flu during the inspection week. No one believed him and it took him a while to recover his credibility.
- If you've had very positive feedback from an inspector, I wouldn't mention it in front of colleagues who haven't.
- Skipping lunch won't enhance your performance in the afternoon. Take a proper break with a decent meal.
- Missing sleep. If you are used to a healthy social life it is worth curbing it for a week or two. You can always make up for it later.

Interacting with the inspectors

- As a group, teachers should impress on the head diplomatically that the inspectors are not needed in the staffroom. Most heads are amenable to setting aside a room for them, and arranging for the tea to be delivered and leftovers removed at the end of each break, so they have no excuse to enter the staffroom, because the teachers need a sanctuary where they can cry and swear in peace.

- If one of the enemy enters the staffroom before the end of the inspection, any teacher present should stand up, smile kindly and say pleasantly but firmly, 'Your room is along the corridor, I'll show you where it is'. Open the door and look them in the eye until they leave. They are unlikely to stay but, if they do, teachers should make sure you complain to the head that the staff's personal space has been invaded.

- When inspectors arrive in your classroom to observe your lessons, smile and make them welcome. It gives the impression you're capable and confident.

- No matter how friendly the inspectors are, you should never become familiar with them or drop your guard. Do not mistake friendliness for friendship. Remember they are inspectors there to judge you, not to make friends. Be courteous and cooperative and at the end of the lesson feedback/interview, thank them and leave them.

- If an inspector causes you any undue grief during the week – interrupting a lesson, opening your cupboards or drawers without your permission, being aggressive – make sure you write down the details and pass it to the head. It gives him/her ammunition to throw at the registered inspector in their daily meeting. It is useful for the head to be able to dent their confidence before they start denting his/hers.

Getting your grade

Teachers tend to set high standards for themselves. If they score 'satisfactory', they often feel they've underachieved, as if the grade was 'unsatisfactory'. Try not to fall into the trap of setting impossibly high standards for yourself. You probably spend all day encouraging pupils and building up their self-esteem, so don't undermine yourself.

If you get a grade of satisfactory, be happy about it. If you do happen to get a grade of unsatisfactory, don't worry, we're all allowed one. Remember each lesson is only a single frame in a very long film. There's no need to tell your colleagues if you don't want to. Unless they've heard a rumpus emanating from your room, they have no way of knowing.

Combining Ofsted with running a home and family

Make sure you have the support of your family. I ask mine not to expect much sense out of me for a few weeks until it's all over. If your children are at school, explain to them that this is examination time for you, and you need extra time to yourself to prepare for it, so you might not be so available to read them stories, help with their homework and play Monopoly for a few days/weeks. You can soften the blow by promising a treat like a trip to the cinema or a theme park at the end. You will need it as much as they will.

Try asking your partner and grown-up children at home to give extra help with the cooking and shopping until it's over. A colleague who was a single parent of a young child fed her family with take-aways for a week, to reduce the pressure. Ignore the feelings of guilt. Remember your being a proficient teacher who can earn a salary enhances the quality of their lives. You are important and you must take care of yourself.

Getting a good night's sleep is vital to you. If you have small children who wake you in the night, you must persuade your partner to attend to them. If you have older children who need you to help them with homework, you can appeal to their better nature in advance, by warning them you'll need to be in bed early that week because you have to cope with being examined the next day. It is also showing them the importance of getting to bed early in an examination period.

Whatever your situation, don't let yourself get run down. We all need something to keep ourselves feeling on top of the job. Whether it's an evening at a yoga class or the local gym, a night in the pub with friends or simply regular vitamin pills, you must insist on finding time to look after your own wellbeing.

When it's over, indulge your family for a week or two to show how much you appreciate their support. Leave school as early as you can after the pupils go home so you can devote yourself to your family. Remember you may need to call on their goodwill in two or three years time, or less if you move schools.

Preparing for interviews with inspectors

During the week you'll probably have to suffer an interview with one of the inspectors. Remember your manner is almost as important as the answer. Hold your head up, look them in the eye and smile. If you don't know an answer, don't balk. Smile confidently and say, 'I'm not sure about that. I would be interested to hear your suggestions'. I once said that to an inspector during an interview and he changed the subject.

Forewarned is forearmed so start preparing essay type answers to the following.

Questions likely to be asked of a support teacher for special educational needs or English as an additional language. These can apply to either primary or secondary.

1   How do you assess a pupil's needs?
2   How do you decide which pupils to target?
3   How do you monitor their achievement?
4   How do you prevent failure?
5   How often do you confer with parents?
6   Explain your record keeping system?
7   What role do you play in planning lessons with the class teachers?
8   What criteria do you use to set targets?
9   What else do you do to enter into the life of the school? Assemblies, school trips, after-school clubs, school journeys?

If you have a post of responsibility

If your school has not been inspected in the previous two years, it's worth finding the latest document on your subject, written by the Department for Education and Skills, **before** you're notified of the inspection date. You couldn't possibly read it all. I've not met many who have. Just pick out main bits to refer to in the interview, so that you sound up to date. In case the head or head of department gives you no guidance, plan answers to the following.

1   How often do you monitor the work in your subject, in each year group?
2   How do you assess progress and how often?
3   How do you keep the curriculum under review?

4 How often do you give Inset to the staff? What topics have you covered since taking up your post?
5 How do you organize your record keeping?
6 What changes/improvements have you implemented in the time you have had your post?
7 May I see your development plan for the current year? How much of it have you completed so far?
8 When did you last write a school policy for your subject? (Have a copy available.)

Providing answers may seem straightforward, but some teachers interview badly because they are nervous or ill-prepared and don't remember all the details until three hours afterwards, when they're drowning their sorrows with a few drinks. As with job interviews, write out the questions and model answers and read them over before the interview. Ask a friend or partner to give you a practice interview beforehand. It always builds up confidence.

If asked about an issue with which you've not yet dealt, try not to become tongue-tied or feel caught out. Smile confidently and say smartly, 'That is one of my targets for next term,' or, 'I have not got round to that yet because . . . has been a more pressing priority'.

Junior members of staff
You are less likely to have an interview but it's wise to be prepared. If postholders and heads of department have not given you a list of likely questions and answers for your subject(s), just ask them to suggest a few likely questions and confirm that your prepared answers are appropriate. If they're not able to offer any suggestions, try preparing answers to these. They can apply to primary or secondary.

- How do you organize your class(es)?
- How do you plan your week's work?
- What strategies do you use for assessment?
- What discipline strategies do you use?
- How do you support your pupils with special needs/English as a second language in class?
- How do you assess which pupils to place on the special needs register?

What a competent head does afterwards

Some heads are very competent at managing people, keeping their morale up during the days of torture and keeping them on board afterwards. Watch your head to see how many of the following s/he does.

- When it's over, thank the staff profusely for their efforts, and make light of any mishaps which took place. I'm sure it decreases the number of staff ringing in with a sickie the following week.
- When s/he is giving the staff the initial feedback, emphasize the inspectors' positive comments and play down the negative.
- If the school passes, emphasize that there won't be an inspection for another two/three/four years, whatever they decide. It sometimes stems the tide of teachers leaving.
- Provide the staff with a treat, like a catered buffet lunch, by means of appreciation. If the staff feel that their efforts are valued they continue to work hard after they've recovered from the experience.

You can judge how competent the head is at supporting the staff, keeping their morale up and fostering a happy atmosphere by noting how many of them s/he carries out. It will also let you see how important these points are when you, yourself, become a head.

The initial feedback

As soon as the week is over, the head has to confer with the registered inspector and receive a run down of the week's findings, judgements and issues for further development. They then relay that to the staff and await the fully completed written report, the writing of which, I am pleased to say, usually spoils the weekend for the inspectors. An inspector said to one of my colleagues on the final day, 'You know we will have no weekend off. We'll be spending the whole two days typing this up'.

She grinned and said, 'Aw shame. Tell someone who cares!' This teacher spoke from the secure position of knowing that she had scored a high grade for each lesson. It would be unwise to push one's luck with a remark like that otherwise.

The aftermath

After it's over, teachers experience a whole plethora of feelings and emotions – relief, depression, elation, exhaustion, anxiety and a sense of being drained. Even the most competent and hard-working teachers find it absolutely impossible to keep their enthusiasm and energy up until the next mid-term or end of term break.

There's no need to try to be superhuman. There is always a lull before everyone pulls themselves together to write the post-Ofsted action plan. Don't feel you're copping out if you resort to using a few educational videos and fun activities in the next week or two. I know a teacher who was asked by a pupil, 'Why have all the teachers been giving us wordsearches since Ofsted finished?' And that was not even in a challenging school!

Sometimes, during Ofsted, staff irritate each other and on rare occasions they fall out. Whatever has happened during the previous few days or weeks, wipe it from your memory and start afresh. Remember you have to work together.

Go out every night for a week, treat the family to thank them for their support, and don't bother doing much preparation. Just wing each lesson the following week: it helps the stress levels to subside and helps you return to normal sooner.

The report

This comes a few weeks later when you're beginning to recover. The new format may reduce it to as little as three weeks. Most teachers turn to the parts that involve themselves and read that first. There is a tendency among teachers to only see the negative elements, miss the positive comments and feel dismayed. If you find yourself doing this, try highlighting all the positive comments and this will make you feel more satisfied.

If you find any comment with which you disagree don't be afraid to air your views. Produce evidence if you can and pass it to the head to support him/her in the discussion with the registered inspector.

I know a formidable head who received the report, went through it with a fine tooth comb and picked out every point which he could challenge. He looked up evidence to support his points, and gave the registered inspector a headache in disputing each point when he came for the post-Ofsted visit. He persuaded the inspector to retract over 50 criticisms!

If you find yourself working with a head like this one, thank God for it! Unless you're very ambitious, this alone might be enough reason to stay in the school because articulate, supportive heads like this are like gold dust to a pressurized teacher.

Conversely, the criticism may well be accurate, in which case you just have to accept the recommendations and apply yourself to making an input to the post-Ofsted action plan. Don't feel hurt by criticism. It's not personal. Similarly, unless the school has been put into special measures there's no need to be dismayed by the length of the issues to be addressed. Even if the school is classified as 'outstandingly successful' there's still a list of improvements to be made.

It will stand to your credit if you show that you're willing to learn and grow and extend your skills and experience. Making a constructive contribution to any form of school or self-improvement will always raise your status within the school.

17 Special Measures and Fresh Start

Special Measures – every head's dread

When a school fails its Ofsted inspection, it is put into Special Measures. In some cases this is the death knell for the head. Those who don't resign of their own freewill are often persuaded to go. There will be pressure from the parents, governors, the LEA, or the teachers themselves may have a vote of no confidence which would leave the head's position untenable.

It is then up to the governors to select a new head, and the staff and new head are then left to pick up the pieces and restore the school to an acceptable level of achievement. Everyone is given the report setting out the school failings and allowed 40 working days to draw up an action plan to improve the situation.

Fresh Start

A 'Fresh Start' school is one which has failed its Ofsted inspection so badly that the LEA decides to close it down and re-open it with a new name, new head and deputy head. Really, Fresh Start is a euphemism for 'it can only get better'.

Obviously this action alone would have little effect on any school. The new head and deputy need to be dynamic, determined, inventive, well-versed in the curriculum and highly competent in managing both staff and pupils.

The school is left alone for three terms to pull itself up and then they are inspected by Her Majesty's Inspectors (HMIs) for two days each term until they have a satisfactory Ofsted inspection. Fresh Start schools are given extra money to help them improve.

I worked in a Fresh Start school and am proud to say it is one of the few which managed to throw off the Fresh Start label in less than two years. The experience taught me many things.

So what happens to turn a failed school around?

If you find yourself working in either of these, unless you're the head or a senior member of staff, you'll not have much say in the many changes about to take place, but your full cooperation will undoubtedly be needed to lift the school up. The aim of this chapter is to highlight the problems and show what is likely to happen.

Apart from the points to be addressed on the school's post-Ofsted action plan, these are likely to be the main problems.

- Staff morale – no one likes to be labelled a failure.
- High staff turnover. Teachers start looking for new posts and this in turn exacerbates the problem because a lot of changes causes more disruption and increases the pressure on those who stay.
- Difficulty in recruiting new staff because everyone knows about the school's status and teachers know they'll face difficulties if appointed.
- The anxiety felt by those who are left can cause friction.
- Restoring the respect of the pupils.
- Regaining the cooperation of the parents who have lost respect for the staff.
- Improving pupil attendance which is often poor. Staff attendance can be low as well.

So how can it be put right?

Some LEAs employ 'superheads' for the purpose of lifting schools out of the wilderness. Every teacher I know who has worked with one of these found them incredibly determined and often successful. So, what qualities does a superhead need? These qualities and skills are needed in some degree by any head really, but a new head taking over a school in the doldrums needs them all in abundance.

- Vision. A clear view of the potential of the school. It's no good being unrealistic, but there must be a clear aim to improve.

- Highly developed strategies for putting theory and ideals into practice.
- Inter-personal skills. Even-handedness, ability to motivate demoralized teachers to believe in themselves and feel valued, ability to inspire loyalty and mould a diverse, disunited and demoralized group of people into a united team.
- Sound judgement and ability to choose competent staff.
- A streak of ruthlessness in relieving the school of the staff who can't or won't perform adequately.
- Behaviour management skills. Positive attitude to pupils and staff, ability to establish a code of practice and a hidden curriculum, firmness, fairness and consistency.
- Thorough curriculum knowledge.
- Determination to succeed.
- Ability to work hard for long hours.
- Economic management skills.
- Sense of humour – it's a rocky road ahead.

The pupils

Behaviour management

Although a minority of pupils deliberately set about destroying the quality of life in a school, they cannot ultimately be blamed for the school's failure because management of a school is firmly in the hands of adults. If it isn't, then it's the adults who are to blame, not the pupils.

Behaviour management often has to be addressed and this means a whole new behaviour policy must be formulated and all staff must agree to stick to it rigidly because pupils are quick to notice inconsistencies and exploit them.

- In many cases only a zero tolerance approach to violent and disruptive behaviour works.
- Sanctions must be swift and effective. Lots of pupils are temporarily excluded and I know of cases where they were sent in cars to their parents' office when the exclusion was ignored and defied.
- In a minority of cases pupils are excluded permanently when the parents ignore the warnings about their son/daughter's behaviour. In these cases it's important to keep a detailed

record of incidents to have as evidence to fight appeals against the exclusion.

- In–house exclusions. Unruly pupils excluded from class to work alone near the head's office and not allowed to go out at break times. Some parents will object but most at heart appreciate firm discipline.

Making it worth their while to conform
- Lots of incentive schemes of rewards for improved behaviour, effort and attitude.
- To improve punctuality and attendance some primary schools award an attractive cup weekly to the best attending classes in Key Stages 1 and 2.
- Secondary schools sometimes offer an annual reward for 100 per cent attendance.

Help for the pupils
- Sometimes the special needs provision has to addressed promptly because the most needy pupils are often the ones who suffer most when a school is underperforming.
- Likewise, the children who have come from abroad with no English. A policy for English as an additional language and a teacher for them is needed at once because they quickly become positive towards a school which supports them, and disruptive in a school where they are left to flounder.
- A homework club can be beneficial to support pupils who cannot yet work independently or do not have a suitably quiet place to work at home.
- Enjoyable after-school clubs help build up a better relation-ship with pupils and if the club is successful it increases the pupils allegiance to the school.

Setting a new tone
Attitudes are difficult to change. Respect of parents and pupils, once lost, is difficult to regain. Even with a new behaviour policy in place it needs perseverance and attention to detail to make it work. It is often the little things which make the difference, as much as the large ones.

The superhead can largely set his/her own agenda. There is much anecdotal evidence about the first weeks of superheads' regimes. All of these help to establish more positive attitudes towards the school.

- Pupils being sent home to change for not wearing the correct uniform.
- Bare midriffs, thongs and unconventional hairstyles and colourings banned. Even staff can be pulled up for unconventional hair.
- School gates locked five minutes after the bell is rung in the morning to encourage punctuality.
- Pupils made to stand up when teachers enter the room.
- Pupils lining up to enter the building.
- Standing behind their chairs in silence before being told to sit down.
- Soothing classical music played as pupils enter the hall for assembly, which always has a proper moral or lesson.
- In secondary schools, classes taking turns to set out the chairs for assembly and put them away afterwards.

I have met a few teachers who resent the 'new broom' approach but many who had suffered under the regime of a weak head appreciate the firm approach, especially if it brings about the desired effect. On the whole, pupils, if pressed, will admit that they prefer an orderly school life with firm discipline.

Even the most able head cannot do it alone. The whole staff needs to be involved in every area, even if it's only to support and encourage each other.

The environment
There can be little doubt that the environment can have an effect on behaviour. The decor of 'failed' schools is often neglected and sitting in a room with paint and plaster peeling off the wall does not inspire creativity or enthusiasm.

Most heads try to improve the appearance of the school by getting the decorators in or replacing furniture that is falling to bits. You can judge the head's care for the school by noting whether s/he refurbishes the head's office, first or last.

The curriculum

Usually several areas of the curriculum need to be revamped and all the staff of each department have got to be involved. There is often an emphasis on producing creative, enjoyable lessons occasionally enhanced with suitable school trips.

More resources often need to be ordered to improve the quality of teaching – sometimes a tedious and time-consuming job if the task has been neglected for a long time. Usually there's extra money available for schools in this position.

The staff

You can't leave it all to the head. All staff have got to be involved.

- Training may be needed for senior and middle management to set out a plan to help the school move forward.
- Teamwork is essential. Competent heads can promote a convivial staffroom atmosphere which permeates the whole school so that all ranks of staff work in friendly cooperation. This is vital to raise the school out of the mire.
- Only competent teachers can bring about success. Any who are unable to cope, or unwilling to pull their weight, are eased out or pressurized out with the threat of a competence procedure.
- Extra staff can lighten the load – trained special needs teachers, English as an additional language teachers if needed and classroom assistants, who have had some classroom training, to give extra support to pupils to prevent failure.
- Some heads are good at staff bonding activities – staff breakfasts, a night out together once a half-term.
- 'Train on the train' – an Inset day in the form of about an hour of an interactive or paired training activity carried out on the way to Brighton/Paris, where the rest of the day is spent in jollification.

The parents

- Establishing positive links with the home is important. Parents support better when they're involved and kept informed. Weekly newsletters to parents and meetings of parents where the head explains the school's plans to bring about improvement, the behaviour policy, the need for parental support and the importance of punctuality all help.

- Some heads like to set up a parents' committee to organize fundraising events, help with drinks at sports day, go on school trips, run after-school clubs and a rota of parents who come into school regularly to hear pupils read. Their involvement sends out the message to the pupils that school is important.
- Often there is a more open-door policy established to keep in touch with parents whose pupils need extra support. It all helps to create a positive ethos.

Working through this difficult time is tiring, tedious and often feels like an uphill battle, but remember, in most cases, Special Measures and Fresh Start are temporary situations. Often during them, teachers and auxiliary staff pull together in mutually supportive cooperation and in many cases, after a year or two, the school emerges with renewed strength.

There is always an up side. If you've worked in a school which has successfully emerged from Fresh Start or Special Measures it will always look impressive on your CV.

18 Supply teaching

For anyone who is new to the UK, supply teaching or substitute teaching (subbing) means being employed on a daily basis without a contract to fill in for teachers who are ill, on compassionate leave, on maternity leave or doing jury duty. This is a popular mode of working with teachers who want flexible or part-time work, such as those with young children or who want to do something else, like writing. For overseas teachers it's a quick way to get into the system.

You are only paid for the days in which you actually work, so you have to save for your holidays or find a summer job. Some find it difficult to cope with constantly changing, but I have met teachers who found it so much easier, that they kept it up for 20 years.

There are two working modes for supply teaching and we'll be looking at the advantages and disadvantages of each.

On a day to day basis

This means going to any school, for up to a week or two at a time, to cover a short-term absence, like minor illness, shorter compassionate leave or jury duty.

Advantages
- You can work whenever it suits you.
- Holidays can be taken in term time when it's cheaper and destinations are less crowded.
- If you find it difficult to fit into the school, you can walk out at the end of the day and never come back.
- You don't have to waste your precious hours attending staff meetings, planning meetings, parents' evenings or after-school clubs.

- In many primary schools, the year group coordinator just hands the literacy, numeracy and other plans to the supply teacher, along with the worksheets as they enter. Likewise, in most secondary schools the head of department supplies you with the day's work, since they usually have the policy that even unexpected absences should be covered by phoned or faxed in instructions.
- You don't have to be in school as early as the permanent staff or stay so late.
- Staffroom politics can be mostly avoided.
- There is plenty of variety.

Disadvantages
The above makes it sound like an easy job, but there is a downside.

- Some teachers don't leave any prepared work so you have to be good at thinking on your feet.
- In a secondary school, you can be faced with a timetable like

Period 1 and 2	Year 9 Woodwork
3 and 4	Year 10 Physics
5	Year 7 Drama
6	Year 8 English

- If you are in three or four different schools each week, your working life can become so disjointed that there's no job satisfaction.
- It can be a steep learning curve – 30 new names every day or two, a new set of staff, a new building to find your way around and often a different set of timings and a new set of working rules. You have to be a fast learner.
- Feeling isolated. Some have told me that in some schools the staff never bother to speak to them. Of course it may be that you disliked the in-fighting and staff politics anyway, so a bit of isolation seems like a blessed relief.
- Some supply teachers are not given enough information. Some permanent teachers think you should learn all the workings of the school by osmosis, as soon as you enter the building. In extreme cases they even look at you in surprise that you did not know all the school's timings and procedures after a day or two in the school.

- You are constantly working to someone else's agenda, and with pupils you don't know.
- Some primary teachers complain that schools take advantage of supply teachers, always asking them to do playground duty.
- Since you are here today and gone tomorrow, discipline can be more difficult because you don't have the opportunity to build up a relationship with the pupils. Some classes see you as a walkover.

Medium–term supply work

This means working in a school for a term or two to cover longer absence such as maternity leave, major surgery, nervous breakdowns and sabbaticals.

Advantages over day to day work

- You have continuity and see progress so it's more interesting and rewarding, and of course the job becomes easier the longer you're in it.
- If you are looking for a permanent post, you stand a fair chance of a acquiring one in that school if you get on well with everyone.
- You may still get the odd day off if you want it.

Disadvantages

In the beginning you have the same disadvantages as a day to day supply teacher but these decrease the longer you're in the school.

- Generally you have to work much harder at this one, as you'll be expected to put time into the time-consuming activities mentioned above. What you derive from the job is in proportion to what you put in.
- If you do not have your own class(es) and are just covering absences or teachers' non-contact time, you can feel like a bit of a spare part.

Think ahead

Before you start looking for supply work, consider your long-term prospects. Agencies do not pay into the Teachers' Superannuation

Scheme for you. If you're living in the UK temporarily or if you intend only doing it for a short time until you find a permanent post, this will not concern you. If, however, you intend doing it for a longer period, say several years or permanently, you must seriously consider taking out a private pension. Otherwise you may find yourself having to work past retirement age.

Also ask about the pay policy. It can differ from one employer to another. It may be a flat rate for all or vary according to your qualifications and experience. Some agencies pay a higher rate for long-term supply, for example more than half a term in one school. At the time of writing (2004) agents quote around £125 per day and up to £170 for their most able/long-term teachers.

Also bear in mind that some agencies ask schools to pay them compensation if they offer a permanent post to one of their staff. This of course varies depending on the agency and how long a teacher has worked for them. I know a head who decided against offering a post to a strong candidate on hearing that there was a penalty to pay. However, an agent admitted to me that he could never prevent a teacher from taking up a permanent post in a school and whatever the circumstances an agency could never sue a school if they refused to pay the penalty. Nevertheless, it is always wise to ask the details in advance.

If you work for an LEA, which keeps a permanent pool of supply teachers, it is wise to ask first if they guarantee work each day and if they pay pension contributions for you.

Ways to find work

Through the LEA
Look in the phonebook for the address and number of your LEA and ask to apply for their supply list. Some LEAs have given up keeping one.

Agencies
In large cities they are usually desperate for staff and I've known teachers to be taken on immediately after being turned down for several jobs. Try the phonebook or the list of agencies provided in the appendix. There are always agencies advertising for staff in the *Times Educational Supplement*.

Directly through the school

Get out the local street map or A–Z and make a list of the schools which would be convenient and then approach them.

Word of mouth

If you know any teachers, ask around. There's usually someone whose head would like a supply teacher.

So how does a supply teacher cope with all that?

A convenient way to do it is to try and become assigned to one school, preferably one near to your home, so that you become acquainted with the teachers and pupils and the school's way of working. You will gain more job satisfaction out of it as well. When you've made a list of nearby schools which you like, dress yourself smartly and call in at each one and ask the heads if they ever need a supply teacher and how often. Give each head a card with your name, address and phone number, tell them you're available and local, and can usually be in the school at 15 to 30 minutes' notice. This is music to a head's ears if they like you, especially in a city where the head has to use expensive agencies for supply cover, because they can save the agency fee as well.

I knew a teacher who was unemployed and having a hard time in finding work, so one day, to lift herself out of her depression, she went into the nearest school and told the head she was a supply teacher with no work for the day and said she would be willing to spend the day, without pay, helping any teacher who wanted her. The head offered her a day's work covering a class with pay. In an inner-city area it sometimes works, but I would not try it more than once in any one school. You do of course take the risk that you might work all day as someone's classroom assistant for nothing, but even that alone might help you to gain a little bit of work for the future.

I found it daunting having to face a secondary age class to 'teach' something I knew little about. Most teachers can manage something in most subjects for Years 7, 8, or 9. Beyond that you do need more specialist knowledge. If you find yourself in this position, and no work has been left, you may have to resort to telling the pupils that they can have the session to read or get on with homework as long as it's done quietly. No one can blame you, if they have asked you to cover a subject for which you have neither qualifications or experience, and no work has been supplied.

Look after yourself – maximize the convenience

- Sign up with more than one agency, so that you can be choosy about where you go and what age groups you teach.
- If you don't want to risk a school lunch, have a packed lunch prepared the previous night in case you get a late call.
- If you get a very late call, say 8.40am for a school which starts at 9.00, don't panic. It is better to turn up late than speed through the traffic. They will be so glad to see you they won't mind.
- Always ask the school in advance what the parking situation is. The school car park is normally full and if there's no street parking, it is best to know in case you need to use public transport.
- If you are new to the area ask advice on how to get there.
- Unless you're absolutely desperate, never go on a journey of more than an hour.
- Ask the agency, where possible, to tell you the day before what school they want you to go to, so you can find its position on the map and work out your route. You can also ring up the head and confirm which year group/s and they might even let you know what the pupils are studying. They will appreciate your interest.
- If you tell the agency you're unavailable on a particular day, they sometimes ring you anyway. If your arrangement is important, for example a hospital appointment, refuse, but if it's casual like lunch with a pal who won't mind too much, it's worth changing it to accommodate a desirable school.

Establishing a favourable impression

- First impressions count. Always look smart on your first day if you don't know the dress code. It might turn out to be a school where you want to apply for a job.
- Look efficient. As soon as you arrive, ask for a written

run-down of the day's timings, assembly, playtime, lunchtime and home time. Well organized schools have an information sheet ready to hand to supply teachers as they arrive.

- Try to get on with everyone. Strictly no staffroom politics.
- Try to be adaptable but if you really cannot follow the plans left, say so and why. Schools are often so desperate for supply teachers, they can be quite tolerant.
- Always mark the books. It infuriates teachers if you don't, and drastically reduces the chances of your being invited back. It's also embarrassing if the head complains to your agency.
- Leave the classroom at least as tidy as you found it. It always irritated me if I returned to a messy classroom after a day out. Stop the last lesson early to give each child a tidying up job if necessary.
- If the teacher has left you a note about the class and their work, always leave a reply. Teachers appreciate human contact.
- If the school is preparing for Ofsted, don't feel hurt if no one has any time for you. It's not personal.
- If asked to do supply work in an Ofsted week, it's well worth doing it. You will be inspected like anyone else, but will not have to bear the consequences if anything goes wrong. If it goes well you will be assured of a warm welcome in the future for having helped them out in their darkest hour.

Working with the classes – lessen the stress

Primary

- A name game is a effective start to the day with a new class to establish a pleasant atmosphere while you learn the names. Write your name on the board.
- Always carry a range of resources in case you're called at the last minute and there is no work left for you. Some supply teachers carry boxes of activities in the boots of their cars. It is worth carrying some interesting story books with attractive illustrations, especially if there are lots of pupils with English as an additional language.
- Keep a bank of ideas for five or ten minute fillers.
- Even if you're only there for a day or two, try to build up a

rapport with the classroom assistant, or anyone else working in your classroom, because they are the people who will help to make the job easier.

- If you're not following the teacher's plan, ask the pupils to work on pages, not their exercise books. Lots of teachers prefer it.
- Develop lots of discipline strategies, class reward systems, circle games and fun activities to finish off the day.
- If you are in difficulty, don't be afraid to ask for help.

Secondary

- Start by telling the pupils why their regular teacher is not able to teach them, and write your name on the board.
- It's worth telling the older classes that you're a qualified teacher – sometimes they think you aren't – what your subject is and why you are supply teaching rather than permanent.
- Sometimes they try to con you into believing they've not been taught to do the work left for them, in which case ask, 'What did you do last? Which page were you on? Let me see the last piece of work in your book'. You can sometimes rumble them.
- If they ask you to explain something which you can't, try a line like, 'I'm sorry this is not my subject. Who's the best person in the class at this?' Don't be afraid to say to a pupil, 'Can you help me out and explain this?' If you can't find the answer say, 'I'll ask Ms Smith and let you know at the next session,' and follow it through.

If it all fails – few supply teachers avoid the occasional bad experience

- No matter how unruly the class is, try to stick it out for the whole day. Remember if it is awful, you don't ever have to return.
- If it is a nasty experience and you decide not to return, ask the head to sign your form and then tell him/her politely why you're not returning. It won't benefit you but I have known cases where the head clamped down firmly on the class after the supply teacher left.

Some of the above may paint a partially bleak picture, but remember supply teaching is normally temporary and the quickest way to find a permanent post. Many supplies end up as permanent teachers in a school, where they covered classes temporarily. It is an excellent way to find a post because you start confidently, already knowing the school from the inside and having built up relationships with the pupils and adults.

19 Peripatetic teaching

I have never liked that word. It rhymes with 'very pathetic'. If you tell someone outside the profession you are a peripatetic teacher, they usually make some quip about how fit you look in spite of your handicap.

'Peripatetic' means going from place to place on one's business. Peripatetic teachers have permanent full or part-time jobs, with sickness pay and pension contributions. They are not attached to any particular school and are usually employed by a central service and have a timetable which sends them to up to five, sometimes more, different schools per week to teach one specific subject. This might be:

- drama;
- a musical instrument – piano, violin, trumpet, clarinet, anything;
- English as an additional language;
- giving support to pupils with special needs;
- cricket or some other game.

To become a peripatetic teacher you must

- have completed your induction year successfully; or
- possess a specialist qualification, like a diploma or certificate, or have relevant experience or demonstrate a knowledge of the subject and an eagerness to learn.

When you're appointed

Sometimes teachers can be appointed on condition that the relevant course is undertaken, part-time, during the first year or two on the job. This can be heavy going, because although you may have regular time off work to attend lectures, the course work and essays will have to be done in your own time. You also have to break yourself into a new job and study at the same time.

Don't even think about this kind job unless you are versatile and highly organized. Two schools, even in the same area, can have an unbelievably different ethos. I once spent two mornings per week in a very informal school where pupils had wide choices of activity and were never forced to partake in anything against their will for fear of causing them stress. In the afternoons I went to a formal Catholic school where classes of 36 sat silently in neat rows and the teacher ruled, OK! On rare occasions, the cane came out of the cupboard (that was in the 1970s), though never actually used other than as a threat. You don't have to have a split personality to be a peripatetic teacher, but if you have, it helps.

Advantages

- It is easier than day to day supply teaching because you see the same pupils and staff every week and eventually build up relationships with them.
- You mostly work with individuals and small groups so there's rarely a problem with discipline.
- Unlike other teachers who work part-time in a school, you do not have to cover classes for absent teachers. Well, hardly ever.
- You can still avoid the politics, staff meetings, staff versus pupil netball and football matches, collecting payments for book clubs, school trips and all that jazz, but if you build up a constructive relationship you are still invited to all their staff parties and Christmas dinners.
- This type of post is valuable experience because you'll be seeing lots of different schools and learning different ways of working.
- You also gain experience of a wide age range. You can be teaching in three different key stages every week. It increases your confidence and looks impressive on your CV.
- You gain a lot of inside information about each school so that if, after a few years, you want a permanent post in one school, you already know if a school is right for you. If you acquire a

post in one of the schools, you will already have built up a
relationship with the staff and pupils before you start.
- If you have the same age groups in more than one school, you
can re-use your planning and preparation over and over again.

Disadvantages

- Changing schools can be very wearing, especially if you have
to do so every lunchtime and you don't have a car or time
to eat.
- Timetables differ from school to school and it can be confus-
ing. I once went to five different schools in a week and had
five different times for starting school, playtimes, lunch hours
and ends of school days.
- There can be less job security than in other teaching posts and
peripatetic posts are often dependent on money being allocated for them each year. You could be given a term's notice,
although many LEAs have a policy of redeployment rather
than redundancy if this happens.

Tips for looking after yourself

- Before applying for a peripatetic post it's worth enquiring if
the post is secure or renewable annually and what is the LEA
policy for staff whose jobs disappear.
- If you work in a small room with individual pupils, it's wise to
leave the door open, especially if you're a man. Sadly, there is
always a possibility that a pupil could make an accusation
against you. Some teachers advise peripatetics to only work
with pairs or groups for this reason.

Practical every day tips

- Even if you are young and healthy, a car is desirable unless
your schools are within walking distance of each other.
- If you've spent your whole lunch hour on a journey from one
school to another and are unable to face an afternoon without
eating, take your sandwiches out in front of the pupils and eat
while you work. If anyone complains, say that you had to

change school at lunchtime and cannot possibly work on an empty stomach. No one can press the issue because everyone is entitled to a lunch break.

- Until you become accustomed to it all, keep a notebook with the names and details of years, groups, door numbers, of all the teachers and pupils with whom you have to work and all the timings for start and end of the day, assembly, break and lunchtimes for each school.
- Unless it's a very small school, ask each school for a plan of the building.

Keeping an eye on the future

- If you intend to return to being a class/subject teacher, it's best not to stay in this job for more than a few years as heads sometimes think you might have lost the knack of class teaching.
- Don't forget the filing cabinet. Keep a copy of every lesson plan and keep an eye on what your colleagues are doing.

Staying on good terms with everyone

- Sometimes teachers try to pump you for information about other schools where you work. It is important to be discreet and never say anything which the staff of another school might resent, especially as you might want to apply for a job in that school one day.
- If you have a resource that would be helpful to class teachers, offer it. It generates goodwill and maintains your credibility as a knowledgeable teacher.

Methods of working

Withdrawing from class

If you teach a musical instrument, you will withdraw the pupils from a class and there'll probably be a system in place for this. Often the school policy is that the pupils do not miss the same lesson each week and so you must be prepared to have a different time-table every time you visit the school. Teachers can be fussy about which lessons a pupil misses so some tactful negotiation may be necessary.

However, the head or staff will probably know nothing about how to do your job so they cannot interfere with the methods you use. This is a lovely job for the teacher who loves to be autonomous.

Working alongside the class teacher

If you are a special needs teacher or if you teach English as an additional language, you will most probably be working in the class-room with the class/subject teacher and have to fit in to his/her structure. If this is the case it is best to feel your way in gently, because some teachers are nervous of having another teacher in their class. I always agreed to anything they wanted for a few sessions until the teacher was used to me and then started making suggestions if I wanted to do things differently.

If you work in partnership with the teachers it is often difficult for you to attend the planning meetings, because you'll probably be off site. You need to at least suggest to the class teacher that you plan for the next lesson before you leave the school each day. They may very well refuse if this does not suit them, but they will appreciate you showing you're willing. You may end up doing what they organize for you without any say in it yourself.

Adaptability is the keyword in this job. Some teachers dislike always working to someone else's plan, but it is best to look on the bright side. You are saving precious time by missing the planning meeting and since it's not your fault, the class teacher will have to prepare the worksheets and find the resources for you.

Taking the whole class for the teacher

I have known drama and cricket teachers to work in this way. They take whole classes for a session of a specialist subject. The class/subject teacher may be there as well or the peripatetic teacher may be left on their own with the class.

Advantages are that you're only teaching one subject, you become proficient at it and it's usually a fun lesson so the pupils are interested. You can also re-use your lesson plans.

It can also have the disadvantage that when teaching whole classes in some schools, the pupils give a lesser standard of behaviour to outsiders. If this happens, you can ask about the school's behaviour policy and ask other teachers who teach the class what discipline strategies they use. In the worst cases you may need to ask for support. This problem often subsides as time goes on and you build up a relationship with each class.

Covering for absent teachers – conflict with the head

On rare occasions a head may view you as a useful extra and try to make you do things which are not your job, for example accompany classes walking to the swimming pool or cover for absent classes. This is difficult as they can make your life uncomfortable if you refuse. If a teacher is suddenly taken ill, it would seem reasonable to stand in if no one else was available, but if the head is trying to use you regularly to save money, say politely, 'Sorry that's not what I am here for'.

If they insist, and they sometimes do, make sure you tell your line manager at the service where you're employed. S/he should support you by speaking to the head to reconfirm your terms of employment. If s/he is unwilling to do so, you may be stuck with it.

If this happens to you, make sure you keep a diary of all the times you have been withdrawn from your work and keep it as evidence to exonerate you from blame if the pupils you should have been teaching have not made acceptable progress.

Occasionally the head tells you to do the job differently from your line manager at the service where you're based. This puts you in the dilemma that whatever you do, you are wrong. I found the best response was to smile and say, 'Will you please speak to my manager about that'. Offer the head the phone number and say, 'I don't mind which way we do it. Discuss it with her/him and I shall go along with whatever the two of you decide'. This type of debate sometimes generates more heat than light so unless you have a definite preference, it is better to stay out of the conflict.

The upside and downside of the job

I have met teachers who have found this a really frustrating job as you have to be ultra flexible to be able to fit into every niche. But, apart from a few interpersonal difficulties, I always found this a really enjoyable job. The variety was great and if you did the job well, teachers were grateful for your help. Pupils often said they enjoyed the lesson because they had someone to help them with their work. If you are new to an area it helps you to make lots of friends as you will be visiting a variety of staffrooms.

20 Support teaching in someone else's classroom

For those from abroad and not familiar with British schools, support teaching is working in someone else's class with the class teacher to give extra support to pupils who are unable to access the curriculum otherwise. Support teachers can be full-time, part-time, peripatetic or attached to one school.

Support teachers work in both primary and secondary schools. Their pupils are often called the focus group. The support teacher usually draws up a list of objectives to fulfil with them during the course of the term.

Sometimes the pupils have special needs which prevent them from learning unaided, i.e. they may be slow learners who cannot keep up with the class but can cope if they have a teacher to go through the lesson with them at a slower pace, frequently simplifying it for them.

Sometimes they have emotional problems if they've suffered neglect, abuse, bereavement, if they live 'in care' or have come to Britain having escaped from a country which is war-torn. These in turn may lead to behavioural difficulties which prevent even bright pupils from learning and enable them to wreck the class.

Some support teachers concentrate solely on pupils who do not speak much English and who may occasionally have special needs or behavioural problems as well.

To become a support teacher you need to have completed your induction year and have a specialism which you can offer. A few years of experience and a specialist qualification enhance your chances of acquiring a post as a support teacher, but depending on supply and demand, neither are absolutely necessary if you can demonstrate knowledge, experience and an eagerness to learn or acquire a qualification.

Posts are advertised in the press, such as the *Times Educational*

Supplement, www.eteach.com and in newsletters and bulletins produced by each LEA. They are normally advertised by the school or a service which employs support teachers, for example an ethnic minority achievement or special needs service, a music or drama centre or a school.

The advantages

These are mainly to do with smaller groups.

- A support teacher doesn't have to cope with classes of 30 all day, every day.
- Less planning to keep you in school for hours every evening.
- Fewer records instead of a full set for each subject or class.
- Much less marking.
- Fewer discipline problems.
- The pupils love the extra help and attention so they usually make you welcome in their class and work well with you.
- A close relationship with your focus pupils is easier to achieve in a small group.

The disadvantages

Problems with the teachers or head

- Although many teachers appreciate your help and make you welcome in their classroom, a few think you're doing the job because you're too old/weak/incompetent to run a class and are not above jibing you about it.
- Some teachers feel threatened by a support teacher in their class, because they are afraid the teacher might be better at the job than they are, and occasionally try to undermine them. A few class teachers have admitted as much to me.
- Sometimes the head sees you as a convenience for covering classes for absent teachers. This is fine on rare occasions but a small number do it regularly.

Problems caused by the nature of the job

- You are constantly changing class and it's more difficult to maintain a relationship with six or seven classes than one.

Secondary teachers do not mind because they expect to do so anyway, but primary teachers often find difficulty adjusting to it.

- You may find that it can be heavy going, only ever teaching one or two subjects to the most challenging pupils.
- You are constantly working to someone else's agenda and have very little choice in what you teach.
- If you're a teacher of English as an additional language, your job can be dependent on funds coming through each year or two. It's an enjoyable job but some teachers dislike the insecurity.

Different modes of working as a support teacher

Schools differ on this point. Each school has its own policy about how the support teacher works in the classroom alongside the class teacher and some have a *laissez-faire* attitude. I found all of these at different times and in different schools.

1   Only the class teacher leads the lesson and works with the main body of the class, while the support teacher only works with the pupils who need the extra support. (This tends to be the option of teachers who are afraid of the support teacher taking over.)

2   The class teacher and support teacher share the delivery of the class lesson and then the support teacher concentrates on helping the focus pupils carry out their task.

3   They alternate teaching the class lesson and supporting the focus group.

4   They divide the class into two equal groups and work separately at the same lesson in the same room. This works well for practical lessons in science and technology which are harder to organize with larger groups.

5   When the focus group just cannot access the main part of the lesson because of their limited ability or lack of English, the support teacher prepares a different lesson and delivers it while the class carry on with their own work.

6   The support teacher takes the focus group out and works in another room. This is the method preferred by class teachers

who feel uncomfortable with another teacher in their room. It is frowned upon in some schools where they believe that the focus pupils are being rejected or excluded, but I found that a lot of the pupils preferred it.

Start on the right foot

It is worth having a chat with the class teacher to establish the ground rules before you start. Ask about the class discipline strategy and classroom rules, and try to use the same because pupils are quick to note an inconsistency and exploit it to their advantage. Does the class teacher mind if you chip in with extra information, while s/he delivers the lesson? Who does the marking? Who do the pupils ask for permission to go to the loo? The last point is not as trivial as it sounds. On one occasion a child asked me while her partner in crime asked the class teacher and they had an unscheduled playtime at the loo for a while before we realized.

If you have been a class teacher you may remember how you disliked anyone interfering in how you organized your class. Although most teachers are eager for your help, a few are wary of you encroaching in their territory. Avoid confrontations at all costs, not least because the head will most probably support the class/subject teacher, because they have the overall responsibility for the class's progress.

To be a successful support teacher you must accept the responsibility for developing a positive, working relationship with the teacher and class. Remember a support teacher's task is to support the pupils' learning, not organize, criticize or waste time establishing your status in the classroom.

Remember you might be working with six different teachers who, even in the same school, want a different combination of class rules.

Fitting in with the class teacher's organization

Teachers' styles and systems of organization are wide-ranging, so you must be flexible and develop a wide range of skills. If the support teacher is determined to bend each class teacher to his/her way of working, ructions will ensue.

In the first few lessons it is worthwhile to fit in with whatever the class teacher wants. When s/he has become accustomed to you, then you can start making suggestions.

Coping with teachers who feel threatened by you

- If class teachers are regularly making comments about you having a cushy job, I always just asked, 'So what's stopping you from applying for a support teacher's job?' That always finished the conversation.
- If the class teacher is the type who is afraid of you taking over, wait for a few weeks until s/he has got used to you and then offer to take the class occasionally to give the class teacher a chance to support the lowest group. The change could be a blessed relief for both of you.
- If you really cannot work peaceably within the classroom with the class teacher, offer to take the pupils out and work elsewhere, even if it's against school policy. If the head or subject coordinator objects say gently that the two of you find it difficult to work in the same room. As long as you do not put the blame onto the class teacher and it does not often happen, you shouldn't be blamed.
- Every time you see that 'I feel threatened by your presence in my classroom' expression on the teacher's face, start admiring the pupils' work on the wall or saying how much you liked the class's last lesson/assembly.

Keep the goodwill and the rest will fall into place

- If it's a primary school and the teachers have to collect their pupils from the playground and lead them back at the end of the session, offer to share the task.
- At the end of term when the teacher is exhausted, offer to take the class for a morning/afternoon and give them a bit of non-contact time to write records, reports, etc. This not only generates goodwill, it maintains your credibility as a competent class teacher and prevents teachers from accusing you of liking a soft option.
- If some of the staff organize an after-school club, offer to do

one as well if you can. Also make sure you take your turn at taking assembly, playground duty and school trips. You only get the same respect and credibility as a class teacher if you show the same commitment as one.

Difficulties with the head

As with being a peripatetic teacher, it becomes tricky if the head regularly wants to use you as supply cover. It is reasonable to do it once or twice a term if the head is really stuck. If the head tries to use you as supply cover on a regular basis, point out politely but firmly that it's unfair because it's not your job, and worse, the pupils who need your support, are losing out. Tell him/her that you have come in with work prepared for those pupils and you will probably not be able to use it again, so it's a waste of your time. You can soften it by saying that you don't mind helping out occasionally, but if it becomes a habit it's not worth your while being there. You may be lucky and the class teachers who rely on your support for their focus pupils may back you up. It is worth trying to enlist the support of the deputy head or the senior member of staff responsible for your subject.

If you're employed primarily by another body, like a Special Needs centre or an Ethnic Minority Achievement centre you can enlist the support of your head or line manager from it. They can threaten the head with removing you as you're not doing the job for which you're paid, and that usually resolves it.

If you are a permanent member of the school staff and the head is adamant that you're more use saving the school money as a supply teacher than as a support teacher, then you have two choices. One is put up with it and the other is to find a new job. If you choose the latter, make sure you inform the governors in your letter of resignation why you're leaving, and tell the local inspector of your subject of your reasons for leaving. Obviously that is not going to do you any good, other than the satisfaction of knowing you have embarrassed the head, but it might stop him/her from treating the next teacher in the same way.

21 Unions and professional associations

For those who are new to the UK and its schools, some background information is important. Unlike some countries, there's a variety of teachers' unions and professional associations for teachers to join. Every teacher has the right to belong to a union or a professional association and equally the right not to belong to one. Each one presents it own benefits to its members, but generally they all provide support if:

- you have a problem with salary;
- you are unfairly dismissed;
- you are being victimized at work;
- you are being made redundant against your will;
- you need advice about pensions;
- you have a difficulty with threshold payments and fighting an appeal;
- a pupil in your care has an accident and the parents decide to sue you for negligence;
- a child makes an accusation of abuse against you and the parents decide to prosecute;
- you are assaulted by a pupil or parent.

The last three points are the most important. One should only join a union or professional association which guarantees full legal cover for each.

Each school and college has a union representative for each organization which has members in it. You might not need the following list, as the representatives of each organization will approach you to canvass your membership soon after you arrive.

The contact details of all of these are in the directory at the back of this book.

- Association of Teachers and Lecturers (ATL)
- Association of University Teachers (AUT)
- Educational Institute of Scotland (EIS)
- Irish National Teachers' Organisation (INTO)
- National Association of Head Teachers (NAHT)
- National Association of Schoolmasters/Union of Women Teachers (NASUWT)
- National Association of Teachers in Further and Higher Education (NATFHE)
- National Union of Teachers (NUT)
- Professional Association of Teachers (PAT)
- Scottish Secondary Teachers' Association (SSTA)
- Secondary Heads Association (SHA)
- Ulster Teachers Union (UTU)

Look carefully at what is on offer from each one and choose that which best suits your needs, never the one with the pushiest representative. Beware of the one who tries to badger you into joining his/her organization. They are not always the ones who give you the most support if you have a problem.

Also try not to be influenced by the size of the fee. It is tempting in your early years to go for the cheapest one but it really is more important to compare the benefits and services of each.

Some have added fringe benefits like access to a legal advisory service or discount cards and some insurance companies give reduced premiums for members of certain unions.

Today we live in a litigation-happy society and a minority of parents view their child's accident as a large pound sign. Some parents threaten court action, some carry it out but few succeed in getting a guilty verdict. Your union should provide you with advice from a barrister experienced in dealing with this type of case and, if the worst happens, a barrister to represent you in court.

If a pupil has an accident while in your care, you must consult your union or association representative in school at once. If you happen to be the only member of that organization in your school, then telephone the area representative. In both cases, they will advise you of the best action to take, depending on the circumstances. The parent has to prove that the teacher was negligent in order to successfully bring a case against a teacher.

Worst of all, pupils now have levels of power unknown to previous generations. If a pupil makes an accusation of physical or sexual abuse against a teacher, the teacher is suspended until investigated by the police. In the vast majority of cases, no charge is brought against the teacher, but it gives you peace of mind to know that if an accusation is made, there is advice at the end of a phone line, and if a charge is brought, again you'll be provided with a barrister to defend you in court.

If you find yourself in this unholy position, it is vital to keep a diary of all the events. As soon as a dialogue with the head or parent is over, write down as much detail as you can remember immediately. Remember, as with pupils, most forgetting of detail takes place in the first few hours. There are procedures laid down for each case, so stay in close contact with your union representative.

If you had to pay a barrister privately, it would knock you back thousands of pounds. Viewed in this light, the £100–200 membership fee paid by many teachers with gritted teeth each year soon loses its sting.

With pupils increasingly aware of how easy it is to get rid of a teacher for a few weeks, or in some cases months if a suspension is ordered, it's hardly surprising that the number of accusations is on the increase. If you still don't want to join either a union or an association, you should approach your insurance company and take out some private insurance to give you legal cover if the worst happens.

If everyone in the school is in the same organization, it puts the staff in a stronger position if there's a problem with management, or if there's industrial action. However, if you don't want to join the same organization as everyone else, you don't have to. You may need to dig your heels in and refuse to do so. You may receive pressure from your more aggressive colleagues who disapprove of your stance, but it really is best to brazen it out, largely because if they can pressurize you from the outside, you can rest assured they will pressurize you into voting with them, when they have got you on the inside. Although they will never admit it, they will respect you more if you stand by your principles, if your reason is a valid one for you. If you let them see you're a strong character, you're less likely to be pressurized on other issues.

All this leads to the thorny question of industrial action.

22 Industrial action

This emotive topic causes much soul-searching among teachers. As professionals they feel uncomfortable going on strike, particularly as it's children and teenagers who will suffer and it rarely brings about the changes desired. The same teachers are nonetheless dismayed and sometimes angry at being given low pay rises, while they see members of other professions enjoy a higher standard of living. Being belittled because they are poorly paid doesn't help either. It is not the purpose of this book to pontificate or preach about the rights and wrongs of teachers going on strike. Everyone has had too much of that already.

The aim here is to advise teachers on how to cope with the events as they happen and to avoid the accompanying acrimony as best they can. When deciding whether to strike, remember to take into consideration that not only will you lose a day's pay for every day in which you're out of school, but your employer will refuse to pay your pension contribution for that day also.

When there's an issue over which a union must decide whether to strike, the law is that all members must have a secret ballot and the decision is made on the majority vote. Obviously, if everyone in the school belongs to the same organization, they have much more power in closing the school down or keeping it open. Where you have four different organizations in one school the chances of them all agreeing is quite small, hence each representative's eagerness to capture the membership of new members of staff.

Even if you hold a minority view, you have no real choice but to abide by the majority. Especially in the case of strike action, you must support it if the majority of your union vote in favour. If you feel you do not want to be in this position in the future you might decide to join an organization like the Professional Association of Teachers, which is opposed to striking in all circumstances.

Conversely, if you feel you ought to strike and the union votes against it, you have to abide by that decision also. It is never worth going out on an unofficial strike because your union does not have to support you in any dispute arising out of it.

If you're the only person in your school in a union, and the only one going on strike, try not to cave in to anyone badgering you about it. Point out politely but firmly that you're acting within your legal rights. If anyone turns nasty, hold your head up, smile and say that you are all at liberty to follow your own conscience.

Similarly, if you are the only teacher who is not on strike, don't be deterred by the teachers who point out that they're fighting for a pay rise for you, and you're not supporting them. Try explaining that they're doing so of their own choice; you have not asked them to do so for you; and everyone has the right to handle each situation in their own way.

Of course in both the above examples you can probably think of more succinct replies, but remember one day the dispute will be over and you still need to work together harmoniously as a team.

Be wary of heads who encourage the staff to go on strike and then say they cannot go along with it themselves. I once had a head who did so and then stood with a cheesy, gloating grin as everyone opened their pay slip and dejectedly noted the cut in pay. It is never wise to trust the sincerity of those who do not follow their own advice.

If you want to go on strike but don't want to go on a march, because you have children of your own or some other commitments, you can probably do so if you explain that you do support the action, but it's difficult for you to go on the march because you'll lose the day's pay and then have to pay a childminder/carer as well. Your colleagues will be so pleased you're striking they will probably be sympathetic.

If you aren't on strike, do not in any circumstances agree to have anyone else's pupils in your class, except your own child, whose teacher is striking. If you don't have your own child in your class, you will have to pay a childminder.

If you are unhappy with your union/association's stance, you can always resign from your organization and join another, but make enquiries before you do so. Some will not accept members from other organizations until a year after their membership has lapsed.

A phone call to the organization in advance of applying is advisable to avoid being in the uncomfortable position of being without any union support.

Also, if you're paying your membership by direct debit originated by the union, some unions are reluctant to cancel your monthly payment and so you have another fight on your hands. This happened to me many years ago and I had to fight quite hard to persuade the LEA to stop making payments to a union to which I no longer wished to belong.

Always stand up to people outside the profession who disapprove of teachers' unions. When people voice their disgust that a union can make teachers go on strike against their will, point out that the decision is made by a majority vote. I used to say that it was a practice called democracy. Labour and Tory cabinets use it to make their decisions. In fact it often happens that the majority of teachers vote against strike action and prevent it from happening.

Whatever your views, stand by them firmly and don't be manipulated by others, but also respect their right to move in the opposite direction.

Remember that when industrial action is over you all have to work together in a pressure-pot environment, and the less acrimony that has been generated, the more quickly peace and normality will return to the school and the less the pupils will suffer.

23 Applying to move to the upper pay spine

For many years one of the criticisms of the system of teachers' pay was that there was little encouragement for competent teachers to stay in the classroom, because when you reach the top of the main pay spine, there was no longer an automatic movement to a higher level of pay unless you applied for promotion. This often results in more administrative duties and less teaching, but if one stays in the classroom it can look like a dead-end job with few prospects to improve one's income.

If you don't want to be a senior member of the profession, applying to be put on the upper pay spine is one way to improve your pay. The teachers' main pay scale has six points, M1–M6. Teachers with qualified status who have reached point M6 may apply to move to the upper pay spine. This process is called moving through the threshold. The upper pay spine has five points, the first of which gives a rise of £2,000. Unfortunately, you have to jump through a number of hoops first.

Some teachers think it's degrading for competent professionals to have to fill in the questionnaire booklet and present evidence to justify their pay rise, and shrink from doing so. I even know of a school where teachers were actively discouraged from doing so. At the worst extreme, in its early years some teachers were pressurized with the view that the whole system was wrong and therefore no one should have anything to do with it.

One of my friends worked in a school where the head deliberately avoided telling the staff about it in the first year it was applied, until it was too late for them to apply for it. Don't allow yourself to be bulldozed by any lofty moral views. This is money we are talking about. You have worked hard and deserve any extra money that is available.

The application procedure

Although the procedure has been changed recently it is still time consuming, but it is worthwhile to persevere, not just for the £2,000 in the first year and £1,000 in alternate years after that, but for the satisfaction of knowing that your efforts are recognized and appreciated.

As long as you've never been warned that your performance is substandard, you should expect to succeed. So go for it. The money is available for all teachers who have reached all the standards so there should be no spirit of competitiveness among teachers in any school.

The application is now an in-house procedure. The head is the adjudicator except in the case of unattached teachers who are assessed by their line managers.

Filling in the form

There is no longer a deadline date, except the last day of August in the academic year, but it would be wise to put the application in as soon as you can in the academic year as you can easily become more tired as the pressure builds up throughout the year. You can download the form from www.teachernet.gov.uk/ performancethreshold. You need the support booklet to fill it in. You can also download the support pack from the website but it's about 60 pages so you may prefer to order it from the DfES Publications Centre on 0845 602 260 or email dfes@prolog.uk.com quoting the reference on the website. It provides examples of acceptable statements so the task has been made easier than in previous years.

If there are several teachers in your school applying, the easiest way is for all the applicants to bring photocopies of the advice from their unions and associations to a meeting, so everyone has a copy of everyone's guidance, and they then go through the forms and brainstorm their ideas of what to write in each section. Everyone makes their own notes and adapts the ideas and information to suit themselves.

We did that in a school I was in, and it lightened the load considerably. Make sure you put lots of details as concisely as possible in every section, so that it is difficult for them to turn you down. When you have finished, remember to keep a copy.

Evidence

Not everyone who applies is asked to provide evidence so it's not worth preparing a folder until you are asked for it. However, have ready in your filing cabinet all the evidence to which you have referred to in your application form.

The following are useful:

- SATs, QCA, GCSE, AS-levels and A-level results of the last three years;
- medium-term plans, weekly plans, individual lesson plans, worksheets you've made;
- details of school trips you've organized;
- details of assemblies;
- details of after-school clubs;
- performance management targets you've completed;
- copies of development plans and action plans for your post of responsibility;
- a copy of any school policy you've written;
- copies of your Ofsted grades and monitoring feedback;
- a list of courses you've been on;
- details of Inset which you've delivered to the staff.

Lists of other possible evidence are available in the support pack.

The decision

The head, or line manager in the case of unattached teachers, must inform the teacher promptly within 20 days of making their decision and return their application forms with comments, and give oral feedback on their decision on each standard.

Unsuccessful applicants must be given written feedback explaining all the reasons for failing each standard. Feedback should be 'sensitive, informative and developmental' so if you're turned down and the feedback is not delivered in the above manner, make sure you write detailed notes on the conversation as soon as you leave the office.

Appealing against a decision

Appealing against a decision to withhold threshold pay is not an appealing experience.

Filling in the form can be a tedious task but it's nothing like the strain of preparing an appeal if your application has been rejected.

If you've never been warned that your work is unacceptable, you should be prepared to fight an appeal, if only to restore your good name and your dented ego.

The procedure

In past years teachers applied to Cambridge Educational Associates who were completely neutral and independent. This is now an in-house procedure, so you present your appeal to the school governors, who have to work with the head, who has turned the application down. This is a difficult position for them because they'll offend the head if they uphold the teacher's appeal and offend the teacher if they don't.

Each school is required by law to have a pay policy which includes an appeals procedure, including a section for application for threshold pay. It must be available to teachers so you should ask for it as soon as your application has been turned down. You then have to notify the head and governors within ten working days, in writing, that you intend to appeal against their decision. They must then set a date for the hearing, normally within 20 working days.

It will require nerves of steel, because you're challenging the judgement, if not the veracity, of the head who has the power to make your life irksome.

You are entitled to be accompanied to the appeal hearing by your union representative or another colleague. It is better to invite your area representative, who does not work in your school, and is therefore not anxious that there'll be repercussions against him/her for supporting you against the head.

Since each school has its own policy it's likely that the procedure will be different for each school, so the following suggestions are fairly general.

Preparing for the appeal

The decision of the governors is final: this is your last chance, so try to give it your best shot.

- Start visiting www.tes.co.uk/tesjobs. Your days in the school are most likely numbered anyway, and if you can escape before it becomes vicious, life can only improve.
- You can apply to your union or association for support – they may have written advice, but the bulk of the preparation can only be done by you.
- Look closely at the school's pay policy's grounds for appeal. It might be different for each school. The more grounds on which you apply, the better your chances.
- Look at the procedures for application. Check that you had the correct notice and a written list of documents which you had to provide as evidence. If not, this is a defence against not providing the correct evidence.
- Look at the written feedback in detail. Has the head stated an opinion which can be challenged? Has s/he got her/his facts absolutely correct? Can you find evidence in your filing cabinet to refute the comments? Remember everything you say must be backed up with the hard evidence.
- Type up all the comments you intend making at each point at the hearing. It is so easy to forget details when you are in a pressurized position and so annoying when you remember them later.

Preparing your evidence

You may be asked to show all the evidence presented for the original application. After that you will have to look closely at the exact points on which you were initially turned down and find as much detailed evidence as you can to overturn those specific points. For the application you probably only presented a few examples to cover each point, but for the appeal you may need full sets.

For example, if the head said your pupils did not make enough progress, you will have to produce the sets of exercise books pointing out the improvement from the beginning of the book to the end. If s/he said your lesson plans were not adequate, you will have to produce the full set for the past year.

- Written statements from previous staff, the more senior the better. If the head has come to the school during the previous two years, and the previous head writes a statement supporting your application, this greatly increases your chances of success. It is more difficult for present staff to support you because it would place them in an invidious position.
- Any favourable reports from senior staff who have monitored your lessons.
- Ofsted grade forms which are favourable.
- Details of completed performance management targets.
- Evidence of effective teaching – medium-term and weekly plans, schemes of lessons, worksheets and other resources you've made, photographs of pupils engaged in practical work, a list of school trips, SATs and QCA results showing improvement from the previous year; and before and after examples of pupils' work showing improvement over several months.
- Post of responsibility – action plans, school policies, assessment procedures, details of courses you've attended and Inset which you've delivered to the staff.
- The wider curriculum – a list of assemblies, details of after-school clubs, fundraising activities, a list of things you've done to support others, for example delivering pupils to matches, helping backstage with productions or the school disco. Any photos you can present as evidence will strengthen your case.

The appeal interview

The good news is that the support pack states that no one who was involved in the decision to turn down your application is allowed to be involved in the appeal. So you won't have to face an indignant head across the table.

You're entitled to have your union representative in the interview with you, so make sure you do. If you're unable to have a representative with you, you could try to have a colleague with whom you've worked successfully, although this is problematical because you are asking him/her to contradict the head and that can place him/her in an invidious position.

You may feel nervous, but try to hide it: it's important that you play the part in a self-assured manner. If you keep your head up, your shoulders back and look everyone straight in the eye, you'll be taken more seriously.

Some points you may be able to use
- If you've been given an incentive allowance by the head, point out that you would not have been given it if you had not been performing properly.
- If the head has made a criticism which s/he had never mentioned to you prior to the threshold application, point out that if the comment were true, s/he would have told you earlier.
- If the head has written that you omitted a task, which you had not actually been asked to do, point it out adding that you would willingly have carried out the task if asked.
- When questioning the fairness of decisions, don't be put down by waffly answers. Say, 'Excuse me, that's not what I asked you,' and repeat the question. If you don't get a straight answer, say, 'Should I presume from your refusal to answer the question that you are not certain of your facts?'
- Has the head written a criticism of you that is irrelevant? For example, that you have not completed NOF training or other courses that are still in progress. Challenge it.
- Has s/he challenged your performance on any task which is not on your job description? Say, 'I can't be criticized for that. It's not on my job description, I only do it out of goodwill'.

If you are alleging that the head is biased against you
- Has the head been uncivil or aggressive towards you at any time in the previous year or two? Put in a short prepared synopsis.
- Was the feedback given in a manner that was 'sensitive, informative and developmental'? If not, read out your notes on the conversation and present Part 1, page 9, paragraph 22 of the support booklet to them with the words 'sensitive, informative and developmental' highlighted.

An appeals procedure is always an arduous task and you will, at times, wonder if it is worth it. If you are certain of your facts, do persevere to the end and all the stress of it will melt like snow on a warm day, when you finally receive your letter upholding your appeal and awarding you threshold pay.

24 Combining full-time teaching and part-time study

After a few years of teaching, some teachers find they need additional qualifications or become interested in a new area of teaching. If you want to extend your qualifications the best method is to work for the same LEA for a few years and apply to them to give you secondment, i.e. pay your fees and give you a year off with full salary while you are doing it.

If you're not able to get a secondment, then you may have to resort to studying at night and working full-time. Having done just that to acquire my postgraduate diploma in special education, I personally wouldn't recommend this form of self-punishment to everyone. If you have a young child, as I had, think twice. Life can become so highly pressurized and stressful, you wonder if it's worth the grief and stress you're inflicting on yourself and your family.

It might be worth trying to work part-time until it is over. You might enquire with your LEA about the chances of your being seconded after a few more years or if you're eligible to apply for some sabbatical time which some LEAs now offer. If you decide to forge ahead and try to work full-time and study, some of the following might help you.

Before you start

- Talk to your partner to make sure s/he knows what is involved. Unless your partner supports you or, you have the endurance of granite, you're unlikely to survive until the end, especially if you have children.
- Steel yourself and your partner for drastically reduced social and leisure time until the course is over.
- It is only worth the extra effort if you have a definite aim, for example promotion, or moving into an area of education in

which you think you might be happier. If it's only for interest, it's worth leaving it until your children have grown up enough not to feel neglected.

Getting through it and staying sane

As in so many other instances, your ability to succeed is co-measurate with your ability to balance your home, school and study commitments. If you have very young children it is incredibly difficult to juggle it all successfully. The following points helped me, and others, to keep going.

Getting the family on your side

- Enlist the sympathy of your children. 'Dad/Mum has homework too and it's got to be finished before the next lecture,' is a good line and sets a good example to them.
- Also tell your children you can't read them a story or play their favourite game because you need to go to bed early because of the exams, etc. This has the dual purpose of setting an example to them. They take more notice of you if you practise what you preach to them.

Getting support from fellow sufferers

- One of the best ways for groups of people studying for extra qualifications to cope is to support each other. Mutual encouragement, taking pleasure in each other's achievements, telephoning anyone who misses a night of lectures, it all helps to keep everyone going.
- Take time out to enjoy the company of other students. Have a party or go out for a meal at the end of each term, or get together with other teachers in the class to take your children to the swimming pool during the holidays. It all helps to get through it.
- Always go to the pub with the other teachers after lectures, it may be the only couple of hours' peace you get in the week.

Organizing your time

- Plan your television viewing carefully and use the video more. Tape the programmes you want to see and save them as a treat to help you unwind after the work is finished. This way you save even more time by fast forwarding through the advertisements and any other boring bits.

- Find a night in the week which is strictly reserved for yourself and your partner/friends to visit the theatre or cinema. Or you could go out for a meal to save cooking. Having something to look forward to helps you keep your mind off the extra pressure.
- When you have exams or a dissertation deadline looming over you, consider asking the cleaning lady to do some extra hours to release more time for you.
- Make holidays a high priority. They help you sort out in your mind what really does matter and what doesn't, and help you to return to the grindstone with renewed energy and enthusiasm.
- On rare occasions, if the pressure of work builds up to a point where you really cannot cope, take a sickie and don't feel guilty about it if you know the stress has been caused by overwork, not laziness.

At the end of the course

Don't let all that effort go to waste.

- Reward yourself and your family with a night out somewhere really special and planned well in advance, or a fabulous holiday to show them they deserve to be congratulated for supporting you.
- When you acquire your qualification and you're earning extra money, plan with your partner, and perhaps your children, a way to use it to improve the quality of life for the family.

25 Combining full-time teaching with child-rearing

If you find teaching tiring when you're single and have no children, imagine how exhausting it can be when combined with parenthood. Single parents assure me that the pressures intensify when you have no partner. It was quite heavy going before the National Curriculum and its accompanying planning, evaluation and record keeping requirements, but it's now more difficult than ever to balance the demands of the job with those of home and family.

The guilt factor

For previous generations of young parents, the received wisdom was that caring mothers stayed at home with their children and only went out to work if they were single or had financial difficulties. This would ensure that their children grew up to be happy, stable and self-assured adults.

Early studies on the subject concluded that infants were happier if mothered by their own mother, but later ones concluded that children of working mothers would thrive if the quality of surrogate care was satisfactory.

Today public opinion has changed and many young mothers feel pressurized into returning to work as soon as they can after the birth. Whatever decision you and your partner make, you should never let others influence you with their strong views or make you feel guilty about it.

I have known many happy, confident children and teenagers whose mothers went out to work during their early years; but also others who were discontent to the point of going off the rails in spite of having had their mums at home with them through their early childhood. Consequently, I cannot believe that having a mother at home permanently is a deciding factor in how a child ultimately copes with life. I can only suggest that you listen politely to the advice of which you will probably have plenty, but do whatever is most comfortable for yourself and your partner.

When your child is ill on a working day, you'll find yourself in a dilemma. If you take paid or unpaid leave, you might feel guilty that you're letting your colleagues down. If you pay someone to come to your house to care for your sick child, you might feel guilty about being a neglectful parent. I always did but now realize that there was no need because unless it happens regularly, most heads and teachers are quite considerate about it as long as you're doing your job well the rest of the time.

If it's a short illness of a day or two the child doesn't suffer as long as the carer is kind and familiar. If your child has a longer-term illness, or has to go into hospital, you and/or your partner will just have to bite the bullet and take unpaid leave.

If you work for an LEA which allows you a few days off per year to look after your own children if they're ill, do use them wisely. On rare cases you might have to stand up to a childless teacher who resents your having them. Counter, 'It's not fair that you should be entitled to more time off than us!' with, 'Well if you feel that way, you can always complain to the LEA and they might change the rules before you have children!' Also point out that occasional compassionate leave is not just the privilege of young parents: anyone can have it to care for family members who fall ill, a family event or religious observance.

Sometimes male teachers suffer more of this flak than women when they stay at home to look after sick offspring, because the men in the staffroom think the wife should be at home looking after the children. However, women teachers with children of their own will usually admire men who accept their share of the child-rearing.

If your LEA does not allow you time off to look after sick children, you might reasonably take a sickie when they're ill if you're going to lose pay otherwise. It is academic because if your child is ill, and you lose a full night's sleep, the chances are you'll soon be unfit to work anyway.

Whether you call it an advantage or a disadvantage, you may not be able to get into school until after 8am, unless your partner can do the delivering of children to the nursery or childminder. Most childminders do not start until 8am and even if you can persuade one to take your child before that, s/he may not be insured until 8am. This obviously makes it more difficult to be well organized for the day's teaching, but don't feel too guilty about it. You will soon learn to cut a few corners and in any case it's only temporary and as long as you put your plans in on time, deliver your lessons properly and are pleasant to your colleagues, most teachers are quite tolerant about it.

Setting up your support system after a new baby

Before you return to work you need to sort out a proper back-up service. Some couples manage to work different hours so they can share some of the childminding. If this isn't possible you need to look for high quality surrogate care.

Minding the baby

A reliable childminder is an absolute necessity. Grandparents are ideal, but don't like to be taken for granted. It is best to ask first, giving them the opportunity to refuse with a clear conscience. Often they have had enough of child-rearing, after bringing up their own children, and they don't want to start it again. Don't assume they're available: remember they have lives too.

The advantages of having grandparents is that they mind your child for little or nothing, they don't demand extra payment when you're late, or complain when you change arrangements at the last minute, and you don't need to worry about your child being properly supervised while you're working. If they agree, they are probably doing it for love more than money, so it's probably fairer if you only leave the baby with them part-time.

If grandparents are not available, finding a childminder by word of mouth or personal recommendation is probably best. It can be heart-wrenching leaving your child with a minder at first, so if you can find one who has satisfactorily taken care of children you know and like, it sets your mind at ease.

When you first visit, it is best to take the baby with you to see how s/he responds to the minder. It is tempting to just use your own intuition about whether the home has a happy, caring atmosphere but it's wise also to ask to see their most recent inspection report and check that s/he is registered with the local council. Ask questions about their daily routine, and ask for names and phone numbers of past parents, so that you can contact them to take up references. Also you might want to note if the home is clean, safe, well-ventilated, and if there is cigarette smoke in the atmosphere.

You might be lucky and find a minder or another young mother who is willing to bring her own child to your home. If you choose this route, make sure she is registered with the local council. This maximizes convenience for you, because you don't have to deliver your child to and from the minder's/nursery and it saves you the unpleasantness of taking your child out in the cold in the winter. It is also comforting for your own child to have his/her own toys and books around all day and a playmate as well. Of course it is bound to be more expensive, but I have known a few parents who found it well worth it.

Some LEAs are so desperate for teachers that they run nursery schools and crèches for their pupils. These are usually expensive, but have high quality care and qualified staff. Parents tell me that although safety issues are addressed carefully, very young babies pick up lots of germs and become ill. Some parents suggest not sending babies to nursery until they are several months old and they have a better developed immune system.

The cleaning lady

The next requisite is a cleaning lady, unless you enjoy housework, and who does? Teaching is so tiring and your children may have missed you during the day so they'll appreciate your attention in the evening.

Don't even think about doing your own cleaning, even during the school holidays. While she's hoovering and ironing, relax with a cup of tea or play games with your children. Bonding with your sons and daughters is a much better use of time than cleaning the house, and you'll enjoy feeling pampered.

You can often find a cleaning lady locally by asking around people who live in the area. Again personal recommendation is reassuring. If not, you can often find one through the small ads section of the local paper. Most people I know who advertised were inundated with replies. 'Nosy boards' on shop windows, super-markets and library advertising boards are another useful source.

If your cleaning lady is honest, efficient and reliable, treat her with great kindness and give her a pay rise as soon as she asks for it, because she might go off and find a decent job. Always remember she might save you from reaching a state of collapse when the pressure mounts up at examination time and the end of the school year. Having her to work for an extra session in the last week of term is money well spent.

The babysitter

As soon as you return to work, start looking for an evening baby-sitter. Again grandparents and young uncles and aunts are ideal, but if not available there's usually a young neighbour who is eager to earn some extra pocket money.

Some suggest asking older students from your school if you teach in a secondary. I would not recommend this option at all. You won't want one of your students nosing around in your home, and if one of you has to deliver him/her home afterwards there are too many risks involved.

In some areas there's a babysitting agency. If using one, you'll be bringing a stranger into your home to look after your most priceless possession and your other belongings. So it's wise to ask for the phone numbers of other parents for whom the babysitter has worked before.

Remember all that slavery to the National Curriculum and parenthood could turn you into insufferably dull company, so think of the comfort of others and escape for a night out occasionally.

Network support

Before the baby is born make sure you go to an anti-natal class to make friends with the other new mothers. Stay in touch afterwards because you can all support each other by minding each other's babies occasionally, swapping anecdotes for a laugh and giving each other handy hints. Remember your friends who don't have children will find the baby conversations excruciatingly boring after about 15 minutes.

Getting back to work – when and for how long?

Unless you really need the money, I would try putting off returning to work as long as possible. New babies are hard work and you'll be surprised how much it wears you out to have less sleep at a time when you need more. It can also be irritating to return from work and find that your baby has said his/her first word or taken his/her first step and you've missed it. Here's a few thoughts to ease the pressure at this demanding time.

- Consider returning to work part-time to start with. It breaks you in gently.
- Aim to work as close to home as possible and choose your childminder or nursery to minimize travelling time, so if you get a phone call to say your child is ill, you can get there fast. You might be constantly running into your pupils and their parents, but it can be an advantage because some parents like to think of their child's teacher as being a member of the community.
- The early period of your child's life is an ideal time to be a supply teacher on a day to day basis. You don't have to worry about planning, staff meetings and all that jazz and you can have a day off each time the pressure builds up. It is worth cultivating a relationship with a few local heads for a year or two.
- To get supply work, you can deliver your CV in person to selected local heads. They will remember you better after a meeting. Emphasize that you can work if called the night before to give you time to organize the childcare.
- Letting the parents of your pupils know that you have children of your own increases your credibility as one who can understand and cope with children.

Balancing the needs of home and school

Much of the advice which follows can be found in books or articles dealing with a career and a family, but it could be just as helpful to single men in their first job – teaching or otherwise – if they want to maximize their spare time. Saving money is not necessarily the most important issue. Spending more to save you time and reduce stress is more likely to improve your quality of life.

Being organized is the key to coping. There are plenty of ways to save time and energy.

Making the best of the technology

- If you go to work on the train you can save time by using a laptop, compatible with your school computers, to prepare work while travelling, or at home while the children are in bed.
- Online shopping from the supermarket is a boon for saving time and energy. Some websites show you the stores' bargains for the week so you don't miss out. You can also use it for buying books, music, household things, Christmas/birthday and wedding presents.
- Get broadband as soon as it comes to your area. I was amazed how much more quickly I could get through the Internet with it.
- Mobile phones are no longer a luxury. Being in touch by text is cheap and convenient. It is worth buying your older children one each so they can text straight to you when they'll be late home.
- A microwave and a freezer are essential where two parents are working. Cooking meals in batches and freezing for a future evening saves time and it's much healthier than junk food. Microwaves give your teenagers the flexibility to turn up for meals when they please.
- A dishwasher. It's worth the expense to save time and hassle.

Establishing a routine

A regular routine is time-saving and it's good for the family to know where they are with everything. With your partner, sit down and discuss a weekly routine to organize the division of labour evenly to fit in with your working lives.

- Decide what the cleaning lady does and write down all the other jobs – batch cooking to freeze, preparing the evening meals, bottles and packed lunches, laundry, delivering and collecting children, helping them with their homework or bedtime stories.
- Some couples find it easier to allocate one or two regular slots in the week to get the chores done.
- As your children grow older give them each a little job, like filling and emptying the dishwasher. It's always worth a little extra pocket money to both you and them.

- Remember the routine is a servant, not a master. It doesn't matter if it's broken occasionally.

Get your priorities right

Among parents, particularly mothers, there is a tendency to put children's needs above their own. Remember that as parents you are both of supreme importance to your family, and so it's necessary to look after yourselves in order to be fit to look after them properly. Get your priorities right. Yourselves first, family second, and school work somewhere after that. Remember, the school will go on whatever happens, but you and your family need proper nurture and care to remain healthy and happy.

The following helped me to stay on top of it all.

- A healthy diet. No matter how busy I was, I always made certain I had a proper breakfast and sat down at lunchtime for a tasty meal. You will be more efficient and patient if you are not hungry. Don't worry about your weight, you will work it off in nervous energy.
- Sleep is another under-rated issue. Don't try to cope with less than you need. If the washing up is not done, go to bed and let it lie another day or two. Occasionally it won't matter if the marking is left for another day.

When is the right time to be ambitious?

Taking on posts of responsibility is a dubious advantage during this period unless you really need the money, or you're in the awkward situation where you are expected to take extra responsibilities, whether you're paid for them or not.

If you're thinking of applying for a post, it's a sensible idea to study the job description closely and work out how many hours of extra work per week it involves. Then look at the extra pay, estimate how much will be left after stoppages and divide the residue by about 50, to find how much better off you'll be each week. You could calculate the net hourly rate of profit and then decide if it's worth applying for it.

If you decide not to apply, you then find that younger and less experienced colleagues become senior to you in the pecking order.

There is no need to let this trouble you. You are only losing status. As long as you are a competent teacher your credibility will stay intact and that is more important.

I have known many who waited until their children were older and more independent before applying for promotion and then went on to be successful deputies and heads. You can ultimately have both and I'm inclined to believe most cope better if they wait until they're more mature and under less pressure on the home front.

Time management

- When your children are very young, cut your extra-curricular pursuits out completely, unless it's on your job description. If the head objects, tell him/her you will restart them in a few years time when your children are older. It sounds polite and cooperative without actually yielding.
- You won't want to hang around school after the pupils have gone home, so it usually means spending breaks and lunch-times working and bringing the rest home to do when your children are in bed. This maximizes the time you spend with your children, but don't push yourself to breaking point, stop for breaks occasionally too.
- Try to find a time on the weekends when the family can have a treat like a trip to the cinema, or if you are short of cash, something free like the local park or museum. I always found a family visit to the local swimming pool was an effective stress-buster.
- Giving your children a happy childhood does not necessarily involve spending a lot of money. Playing cards, teaching them to make chocolate crispies, sharing time in the library and doing jigsaws together are cost free and help to compensate children for all the time spent away from them.
- Christmas can be a highly pressurized time. If you have a large family circle and need to buy lots of presents, it is lethal to leave it to December when the shops are packed and you're more tired because it's the end of the longest term. Try buying your Christmas (and birthday) presents at convenient times throughout the year and have them all wrapped and

labelled by the end of the October half-term holiday. If you send a Christmas letter with your cards, it is time-economic to sort these out then as well.

Crisis management

Most parents, especially single ones, who teach, admit that it's impossible to keep all the plates spinning at once. All admit they cut corners for a few years when their children were little. This may sound unconscientious but it is a view I have heard expressed by some excellent teachers with happy, well-behaved children.

- If you feel snowed under with too many jobs, then revert to writing down two lists; absolutely necessary and not so necessary. Try to complete the first and dispense with the rest.
- You need a spot in the week for serious de-stressing. A night class on something completely different – woodwork, yoga, tai chi or basket-weaving is a soothing two hours in the middle of a frenetic week.
- If the pressure becomes too much and you need, on rare occasions, to take a sickie, spend the entire day at home if you work locally so that you don't run into your pupils or their parents.

Watch out for the warning signs

Sadly, nervous breakdowns are increasingly a feature of our 24/7 lifestyle and the teaching profession has not escaped. If you're suffering from repeated loss of sleep, poor digestion, becoming increasingly short tempered, feel like crying much of the time or your health is deteriorating, you may be coasting towards serious ill-health.

Sometimes people are so overwhelmed with trying to cope with each day that they don't notice what is happening to them until a colleague or the head tells them. If you find yourself in this position, stop what you're doing and go to the doctor. Sometimes a short period of time off can prevent a longer and more serious illness.

Keeping everyone sweet, including the head

When my children were small, I found the best head to have was a woman who has had children of her own and had to work through their childhood. The worst is a man who believes that you should be at home with your children.

I had a male head who invited himself to my home while I was ill and told me that my child, then 2½, would probably be a juvenile delinquent because I went out to work. A few weeks later, he asked me to give my son to someone and go on a school journey for five days, and was quite taken aback when I refused.

Chauvinistic heads sometimes come over heavy when thwarted. The fastest way to end the argument is to reply, 'My husband wouldn't allow me to do that'. They can't argue because they believe a woman should always be doing what her husband says.

Yes I know it is disgracefully unfeminist, but you need peace at any price, and this is a book on **survival**, not women's rights. My son is now a Cambridge graduate and a teacher, so some might argue the head was right.

If you're a man, and the head is trying to persuade you to go on a school journey, you can look apologetic and say, 'Sorry, my wife can't cope on her own with the kids'. This might sound like I disapprove of school journeys. I don't. They are an important part of a child's education, but unless it's on your contract, you're quite justified in withdrawing from them until your child is old enough not to be upset by your leaving for a few days.

Try to include putting your lesson plans in on time in the list of necessities. It reassures the head you're completing the work efficiently, and s/he will check up on you less often.

If you have the problem of occasionally having to leave staff meetings early to pick the children up, apologise politely and go. Ignore the head giving you a dirty look. It's better to irritate the head than the childminder, as she is more difficult to replace. If you're a man and the head objects to your taking a significant role in child-rearing, smile apologetically and say, 'My wife works so hard, I can't leave it all to her'. It won't cut much ice with a chauvinistic male head, but the women on the staff will love you for it.

Try not to keep saying how tired you are or how difficult it is to manage, because you sound like a whinger or one who can't cope. It also gives the head ammunition to throw at you. It enhances your credibility if you stay tight-lipped about it.

Those of us who have done it, know that it's virtually impossible to put as many hours into the job as you could before the children were born. If challenged, you can point out that it's the quality of work which counts, not the number of hours on the job. You can also add that being a parent makes you a better teacher because it gives you an insight into the feelings of children, teenagers and parents.

The fatigue factor

Whether you're a father or a mother it's incredibly difficult to cope with your first year of teaching during the first year of parenthood, unless you have a first class, built-in nanny. Your whole world changes when you become a parent and you'll be so overloaded with responsibilities. You will need extra sleep and you normally get less. If the baby awakens you a lot during the night and you go into class next day with a drummer practising inside your head, it sometimes helps to appeal to the pupils' better nature.

When my daughter was a few months old, I said to my class one day, 'Please work quietly because I had very little sleep last night. The baby kept waking me up'. The result was the quietest morning I had had all term, so I said it once a week after that.

When we were both working, my husband and I took turns in getting up in the night and early morning for our child who was an early riser. It worked well and created a happier atmosphere since the burden was evenly shared.

For many people, male and female, these are the most highly pressurized years of their working lives. There are times when you wonder how your life can have changed out of all recognition and if you're ever again going to lead a normal, relaxed life. Take heart. Every working parent has experienced this and as the years pass it does become easier. You both become accustomed to it and the children become more and more independent as the years pass, until one day they leave home and all of the early years of pressure and stress disappear.

You might miss them when they leave home, but they're never far from their mobile phones. It is sensible to keep on working as long as you can after they go, because money is great stuff for keeping you in touch with your children.

26 Teaching in a school where your own children are pupils

When your own children reach school age, you may have to decide whether to send them to the school where you work. In some schools it's school policy not to allow parents of pupils to work in the school, but in others it's encouraged because it can be interpreted as a sign that the parent has faith in the school. Some heads also believe it encourages the teacher to stay in the school if their own children are there also.

Many teachers work in the schools where their offspring are pupils and never have any difficulty, but a minority have to cope with occasional irritations. If you know in advance what they might be, it's easier to avoid them, or at least to be ready with an answer. There are clear advantages and disadvantages to having your children in the same school as yourself.

Advantages

- It is more convenient because it cuts out all the to-ing and fro-ing from one school to another.
- If you work in a private school, you'll probably have a massive reduction in school fees.
- If there are any problems that you should know about, you learn about them straight away.
- If your children are ill or have an accident you can reach them quickly.
- You know the quality of the teaching and the school's strengths and weaknesses before they start.
- Possibly without meaning to, teachers give you more regular feedback about your child's progress.
- If your child has a problem, for example dyslexia or dyspraxia, you can make sure teachers do something about it quickly.

- If your children are forgetful – pencils, pens, permission slips for you to sign, you're always there to help them out.

Disadvantages

- It sometimes causes consternation among teachers, who are afraid you're going to irritate them by interfering in your child's education and demanding special treatment. You might find they pester you with advice about how you must conduct yourself.
- Your children do not become independent as quickly as the others. It is too easy for them to rely on you.
- If your children misbehave, teachers complain to you far more often than they would another parent. You are too available.
- If you have to select a pupil for an award for which your own child is eligible to be considered, you have to exclude them no matter how deserving they may be.
- If another teacher selects your child for an award, or a large part in a production, someone might say there is favour being shown.
- In extreme cases a pupil whom you have reprimanded or sanctioned might take their revenge by antagonizing your child – hiding their belongings and silly things like that.
- On very rare occasions a teacher will disapprove of the children of staff being in the same school and victimize one or the other.

The child's point of view

Some children of both primary and secondary age gave me these points but then went on to say that on the whole they like having their parents nearby.

- If something is troubling me, I can always go and find my dad.
- If I forget something or lose something, my mum sorts it out.
- If I'm ill I don't have to wait two hours for one of my parents to turn up.
- I hate having to wait in school for ages for my dad to finish his work at the end of the day.
- It feels strange when my mum tells my friends off.

- Other children tease me saying that I go to the school for £2.50, or I got through the entrance test because my dad works here (private school).
- When mum tells my friends off they tell me my mum's horrible.

Having your own child in some of your classes

If you're a class teacher in a primary school, it's easy to avoid having your own children in your class. Most heads know the problem and are amenable to putting you into a different year group if necessary. However if you're a subject teacher in a secondary school, it's more difficult to avoid your own children, but at least you won't have to teach them for more than one lesson per day and probably less.

Some children love it and some don't. If not handled sensitively, it can spoil a happy relationship. Some pupils play up more in their parent's class than any other. Others become very upset and cry if their parent gives them a rebuke for their behaviour or the quality of their work. Sometimes your child's friends come home to play or have tea and take delight in addressing their teacher by his/her first name.

So how do you handle having your child in your class?

By far the most embarrassing instance is if your child is behaving worse in your class than in others. Of course you'll just have to give him/her the same rebuke or sanction which you would give any other, but at home, in private, it would be worth talking to your child about why they're doing it. Does s/he think s/he can get away with it because you are his/her parent? Is s/he trying to gain street cred with their peers? Is it because s/he feels the need to have your attention above the rest? Try to get to the cause: it's always better than treating the symptoms. Also you have to sort it out fast because your own image is being tarnished.

- If your children come to you for forgotten items, do help them out discreetly, so that others can't complain that your children have any advantage over the others. If you want to tell them to get organized, do it at home.
- It doesn't matter whether your own children call you Mum/

Dad/Mrs or Mr Smith in school. Everyone knows you're their parent.

- When teachers moan to you about trivial things – the sort of thing they wouldn't bother mentioning to other parents – it's tempting to come down heavily on your child. I would try to smooth it over at home in private firmly and then drop the matter.
- If your children complain they have to suffer more complaints made against them than other pupils because you're on-site, point out gently that they also have the advantage of having their parents there when they want them to supply what they've forgotten, or look for their lost football kit.
- Some teachers are afraid someone might think they'll show their own children preferential treatment and so they're more strict with their own. This is not advisable because it spoils your relationship with your children. As long as you are seen to treat them all the same, that is enough.
- If your children are upset by other pupils' reaction to them after a conflict with you, tell them to just laugh and say, 'That's nothing to do with me!' It's best to impress on your children that others will give up if it has no effect.
- If their friends call you by your first name out of school, I would ignore it and the rest of their comments and requests and only answer them when they address you correctly. If it happens in school, I should reply firmly, 'My name is Mr Ali!'

Staff

- When staff start advising you not to interfere, even though you've never shown any sign of wishing to do so, you can quietly ignore it or reply that you had never thought of doing so and thank them for suggesting it; or say that if they're expecting you to do that, they're judging by their own standards. It depends which might work best with the individual.
- If your child is in the dog house try to stay out of it. A teacher in the staffroom once indignantly announced my son's misdemeanours loudly to the assembled company. I replied, 'Well I'm sure a woman of your prowess can sort that out without any intervention from me'.

- If you see a ratty teacher wagging her finger in your child's face at playtime, go and have a cup of tea. S/he probably deserved it.
- If you ever do believe there's evidence that your child is being victimized by a teacher, send your partner in to sort it out.
- Likewise, if you think there's going to be an argument on parents' night, it's easier for the partner who is somewhat detached, and doesn't have to work there next day, to go.
- If a teacher hassles you about what your partner said, interrupt quickly with, 'Well go and talk to him/her about it!'

This can be a tricky situation but it normally settles down after the first year when everyone involved gets used to the situation. In some schools there's a tradition of teachers having their children in the same school and so it causes less friction. You may at times wonder if it's the best way, but before you leave or take your child out, think twice because life becomes inconvenient unless your child is old enough to take him/herself to and from school.

27 Teachers' TV channel

An invaluable resource for teachers

During recent decades a vast number of videos, books and documents have been published on teaching, child psychology, behaviour management and the National Curriculum. There has also been a wide variety of resources to fulfil its objectives. These have been useful to teachers but nothing so far has offered the revolutionary, practical, entertaining and comprehensive service of the Department for Education and Skills' (DfES) innovation, the Teachers' TV Channel. Website: www.teachers.tv

Sponsored by the DfES, it's run by an independent producer, Education Digital, a consortium of the Institute of Education, Brook Lapping and ITV. Unlike videos produced by the DfES in the past, Teachers' TV has complete editorial independence and is managed by experienced commissioners who have consulted widely with chalk-face teachers. This gives the programmes the advantage of a view of the job from the inside.

The channel was formed after a long pilot study of programmes which were produced and shown to serving teachers, heads and support staff. This focus group confirmed overwhelmingly that the programmes were practical and valuable to teachers, classroom assistants, heads and governors.

Programmes are produced by a variety of television companies throughout the country, and have been broadcast on Sky Digital, Freeview, Cable NTL and Telewest since March 2005.

Why have a Teachers' Channel?

The aims of the channel are:

- to set up a channel of communication within the teaching profession;
- to guide teachers in their continuing professional development;
- to bring about school improvement in all areas.

To achieve this, Teachers' TV provides a wide range of stimulating programmes to offer support in all areas of the job and hopefully encourage teachers to stay in a profession which frequently suffers from the loss of its members.

Many of the programmes are inspirational in character, being specially designed to demonstrate all that is creative and satisfying about the job, and may encourage people thinking of entering the profession.

Another strength of the programming is that in schools there's much successful practice which is unknown to anyone outside teaching. One of the commissioning editors told me how working on the channel had made him appreciate what a 'wonderful profession this can be'. Viewing successful work in action may well raise the status of the profession in the eyes of the public, and obviously new teachers benefit from seeing how experienced teachers deal with classroom situations.

We sometimes forget that many parents are unaware of the work carried out in schools. Teachers' TV will have the dual effect of spreading information to them and hopefully increasing their interest and support for their children's schooling.

This much needed service is particularly welcome at this time as other channels have cut back considerably on the time devoted to broadcasting to schools.

Teachers' TV programmes are listed in the *Times Educational Supplement* and television magazines. The channel also produces a wallchart for schools showing a six-week list of all its programmes with times and dates.

Teachers' TV programmes are also available on the Internet, streamed from the Teachers' TV website.

Format

Broadcast 24 hours a day, 365 days per year, the programmes will be repeated throughout the day so teachers will have plenty of opportunities to record them. The programmes are divided into three zones.

- Primary
- Secondary
- General

The Primary and Secondary zones have two sub-sections:

1   Subjects
2   Roles and responsibilities

Subjects

The programmes are short and punchy in style with focused information, rather than long documentaries. They are in hour-long blocks of four 15-minute programmes for National Curriculum subjects. A science hour might look like this:

- a lesson showing effective classroom practice;
- continuing professional development – the lesson is reviewed with discussion on how it could have been improved;
- resources for teachers – producers will trawl the market to show what is available in each subject – a time-saver for teachers;
- pupil programmes – for children to view in the classroom as part of a lesson.

Roles and responsibilities

These programmes aim to give guidance to teachers, and others carrying out functions alongside teaching. They include pro-grammes for:

- headteachers, on management of the whole school including, remodelling, finance and the curriculum;
- NQTs, who have a range of steep learning curves – behaviour management, classroom management, lesson plan guidance;
- SENCOs;

- ICT coordinators;
- classroom assistants.

General Zone

The General Zone deals with issues which apply to both primary and secondary and would be the one of most use to parents, governors and managers. It has:

- a weekly news programme for half an hour dedicated to education news;
- a work–life balance strand called 'Ease the Load' – advice on time-management, dealing with stress and many other topics;
- a career strand about getting on in teaching and improving your CV;
- a strand about the issues involved in taking children out of school;
- 'School Matters' – general documentaries about educational issues such as primary/secondary transfer, aspects of child health, thinking skills, and topical and controversial issues like school uniform and drug testing in schools;
- 'Inspirations' – 15-minute narratives about the successful practice and achievement of teachers;
- 'Just for Governors' – explaining their role and responsibilities, and including improvement plans, setting targets for Governors, headteacher's performance review and organizing contracts;
- a 'What if?' strand where experts in education debate hypothetical and controversial issues, and are quizzed by education writers like Ted Wragg;
- a 'good practice' strand where experts like John Bayley, a former teacher and behaviour consultant, and Sue Cowley, an experienced teacher and author of *Getting the Buggers to Behave* and *How to Survive your First Year of Teaching*, show how they work with teachers to improve their performance;
- a strand dedicated to teachers in special schools;
- other channels' programmes of general interest to teachers.

The Teachers' Channel is the first of its kind in the world, and may be the most exciting and far-reaching project ever set up to help teachers. I have spoken to people involved with setting it up and been impressed with their enthusiasm and determination to make a success of it.

Let us hope that in the future it will become an integral part of the professional development of every teacher in the country.

28 Bereavement in the school

You may think that the strain of coping with several disruptive pupils in one class; arrogant, aggressive parents who are determined to organize teachers their way; or faction ridden staffrooms where staff undermine their colleagues is bad enough. Just imagine trying to stay on top of the job when your school is rocked by the death of a much loved pupil or member of staff.

This can happen at any period in your career: I have known a teacher who had to cope with the death of one of her class in her first year. Few teachers escape this harrowing experience. It has happened five times in my career so far. The beginning of term, especially September, is the worst time to cope with bereavement, because you're deflected from the important task of setting the tone for the term, by having to cope with both your own and your pupils' feelings of grief.

Sadly, bereavement in schools can come in different forms.

- Pupil bereavement – a death in the family is traumatic for a child of any age.
- School bereavement – the death of a child in your form, in any class in the school or a member of staff.

Pupil bereavement

If a pupil in your class has suffered a death in the family, always tell the rest of the class and appeal to them to treat the child sympathetically on his/her return. If the bereaved pupil is actually present, I always send him/her on an errand before telling the class.

Depending on the age of the pupil, if the child is absent some teachers postpone their prepared lesson and suggest the pupils write a letter of sympathy to their classmate. If you do this in a primary school I would break the rules of good breeding and discreetly read the letters to filter out any which are inappropriate before sending them off. Some pupils find this difficult so it might be better to let them write in groups. If the pupils are young, sending a personalized class card made on the computer and signed by each child may be easier.

For primary age pupils, there are some simple but sensitively written books which explore death and the accompanying feelings of anxiety and grief. For example:

- *When Uncle Bob Died* by Braithwaite (2001).
- *Remembering Mum* by Morris and Jenkins (1991).
- *When People Die* by Levete (1997).

Teachers might like to consider if books like these are appropriate to use while the bereaved child is still absent, to enable the classmates to understand what s/he is experiencing. It might make them more sympathetic.

I would be wary of ever using this type of book with a bereaved child present because it might stir up feelings of grief and make the child feel worse. It would only be wise to do so with the approval of parents.

Whatever the age of the pupil, when s/he returns it's worth saying quietly, in private, a few words of sympathy. Make it short to avoid prolonging the agony. 'I was sorry to hear about your Grandma. How are your parents?' This is just long enough to let him know you're sympathetic and short enough not to stir up too much pain. Even if the pupil drops a few tears it's still preferable to letting him/her think that you're unaware of what s/he is feeling or you don't care.

Teachers must also be aware that we're not therapists. Nor can we change the circumstances: we can only help the pupils to cope with them. We can do this by recognizing that the trauma of death can temporarily have a severe impact on a pupil's ability to learn and show more patience and make allowances for late homework and assignments. This may go on for some time because often pupils who seem to be coming to terms with their loss are actually suffering in silence.

Some schools have a school counsellor or have access to bereavement counselling for pupils. It is worth offering this to pupils, with the parents' knowledge and approval of course, but should not be pushed as many people prefer to keep their grief within the family.

If a pupil suffers the loss of a member of their immediate family in the months leading to external entrance exams, it's important to let the school or university admissions panel know. I once wrote such a letter for a pupil who was applying to a secondary school and received a kindly, positive reply. They appreciate being informed and it might swing the balance in your pupil's favour if s/he is on the borderline.

This is a difficult time in any school but fortunately it's usually an infrequent problem.

School bereavement

Below are some suggestions for dealing with this sensitive subject when the need arises. How you'll cope with it will be different for primary and secondary.

Primary

If an infant dies, the rest of the class normally adjust fairly quickly. Their youthful minds are unable to appreciate the enormity of the loss of a child to the family and so they appear to take it in their stride, return to the present and get on with their lives.

If a child in a junior department dies, the older the pupils the more they realize the tragedy of the situation and the more distressed they become. This often leads to difficult and confused feelings among pupils. Occasionally the younger ones laugh at the older pupils (and staff) and tease them for crying. This in turn increases the anxiety and turns the situation into conflict as well as sadness.

If you find yourself coping with this, it doesn't matter if you cry, but at all costs try to avoid allowing yourself to be moved to anger. This fuels the mirth of the less mature pupils and increases the grief of the others who cannot possibly be expected to be mature enough to control their frayed emotions. Try saying calmly, 'Please be kind to the pupils who are upset. This is a very sad day for them'.

Allow the pupils a short time to let their grief spill out but after about ten to 15 minutes try to lift their minds above it by giving them something to do. Make it low-key: it's just to take their attention off their loss. It doesn't matter if they learn nothing that day.

When the grief has subsided, perhaps a few days later, then it's worth explaining that the pupils who laughed are not nasty, just immature and unable to understand how sad Abdul's family must be feeling. Explain that infants and some lower junior pupils do not really understand that death means you will never see the person again. I would emphasize that these pupils are merely immature, not unkind.

Today pupils in primary schools sometimes go to funerals. It is often difficult to close a primary school for a half day for all the staff to attend if a lot of the mothers work outside the home. Sometimes a few teachers volunteer to stay in school with large numbers of pupils while the rest of the staff go to the funeral. If pupils are attending the funeral with teachers it's best to get as many parents to accompany them as possible. In no circumstances should primary school pupils be taken to a funeral without written permission from their parents.

Assembly

Some primary teachers and headteachers handle this extremely well and have an assembly to tell the pupils about the dead pupil's or member of staff's contribution to the school and the community. This is often appreciated by people who worked closely with the deceased, and by the family who should be told about it. If you find this too distressing to attend, you can usually opt out.

Once, after a death of a pupil in a church primary school where I worked, a headteacher told this tale. It worked well to comfort the pupils who felt the loss of a classmate.

Once in a warm pool in the forest a group of larvae lived together. They were a happy group of creatures enjoying a swim together, playing games when the light shone through the ripples, and sharing their food each day. As the days went by they grew bigger and one of the larger larvae noticed that his shell was beginning to crack. He was surprised at this but quite pleased when another started to grow. He found each day that the reeds which he swam round seem to get shorter as he looked to the top of them.

Some of his friends at the bottom of the pool called to him, 'Don't go away, come back down here and play with us'. He peered down the long reed and waved to his friends and called back to them, 'I can't get down from here'.

One day his body swelled up bigger and bigger until it burst, just as he reached the top of the water. He was startled to find that his body had changed. He had a fine pair of wings which he stretched and moved from side to side. They lifted his body above the water and all around was bright and beautiful. He could see the grass and flowers and hear birds singing. He looked down at the surface of the water and called to his friends, 'It's lovely up here, come and see what it's like'.

He folded his wings so that his delicate body rested on the top of the water and he looked down into the pool trying to see his friends. He put his nose on the top of it and tried to go below the surface but it pressed his body back. He tried again and again to pierce the surface but each time his body was pushed away.

Sad that he had lost his friends, he looked around at the trees, and saw some dragonflies gliding towards him. They landed on the surface of the water beside him and when he looked into the water, he saw a reflection of himself and his new friends.

He stretched out his wings and glided away with them, happily knowing that one day his pals below the surface would come and join him.

If you work in a church school or one where there is a high proportion of pupils who belong to any faith which believes in an afterlife, point out that their friend who has passed away is waiting for them in the next world, like the dragonfly.

Secondary

Secondary pupils cope with the situation in a more mature manner, even if they are much more tearful and their distress lasts longer. That is just a sign of their increased sympathy for the family and a deeper sense of loss.

This is no time to be superhuman. If you can struggle through the rest of the day without shedding tears in front of the pupils, so much the better, but if you can't it doesn't really matter, even if you're a man.

Sometimes the head assembles the school to break the news of a death. This is never a tear-free occasion. In a church school and some non-denominational schools there will be prayers for the family. If you have to return to class afterwards, just concentrate on keeping the atmosphere calm. The younger the pupils, the easier it is to cope.

So what can schools do to help pupils and families cope?
It is important to let pupils and supply teachers who are new know who has died and how, and the arrangements for the week in school. Schools are normally sympathetic about allowing pupils to express their grief.

In the days after the death of a pupil some schools make a room, with tea and coffee provided, available for pupils who want to leave their class and sit down and grieve together. Sometimes there's a bereavement counsellor or a teacher available for pupils.

The funeral/memorial service
Before and after the funeral it's important to be sensitive to the feelings of the bereaved family and tell them what you're doing and try to avoid letting the school's grief intrude in theirs.

- In most schools, some of the teachers and pupils will attend the funeral. Sometimes schools put on a coach for the purpose. This helps pupils to get through the grieving process and is always appreciated by the family.
- If pupils have to return to school after a funeral, it's unlikely they'll be in any state to work. Most teachers to whom I spoke to told me they didn't even try to teach pupils at this time.
- Where the numbers are too large to take everyone to a funeral, some schools have an assembly or memorial service in school to remember the pupil and celebrate his/her life. Sometimes parents are invited when the classmates are in the younger forms.

After the funeral
- Classmates often want to write letters of sympathy to the family. If there are large numbers, you can write an accompanying letter adding that you don't want to increase their anxiety by expecting a reply to each. These should be taken by hand to the family a suitable period after the death. If the deliverer is invited in for a cup of tea, it's important to accept as it's seen as an act of care.
- Where there's a write-up about a pupil or member of staff

in a school magazine, it should be delivered to the family, preferably by hand.

- Sometimes schools plant a tree in the child's memory in the school grounds with a plaque commemorating him/her.
- Sometimes a form likes to make an 'In Memory' book about the deceased classmate. It can contain photographs and work done by the pupil and kept in the school library or the form room.
- It is important to remove a deceased pupil's name from school registers and examination lists, etc. at once, so that no one inadvertently refers to them later.

On the anniversary
- Allow pupils the opportunity to remember a friend or teacher.
- Send the parents a card or letter from the school to let them know that their son/daughter has not been forgotten.

Death of a member of staff
Usually the head assembles the school to break the news but sometimes they are unable to do so and leave it to each individual teacher to tell their own forms. When faced with the task of telling my class that two members of the auxiliary staff had died on the previous evening, I deliberately left it to the last thing in the day. This meant that the pupils did not have to cope with the added strain of distress while learning and meant that they could return to their parents for comfort immediately. It also meant that I didn't have to struggle through the day trying not to cry in front of them.

As with the death of a pupil, some may go to the funeral if it's local. If this is not practical, normally representatives from the school attend and the school holds its own memorial service in school or in the local church. In the latter case families should be informed. I know of a priest who telephoned a deceased teacher's family immediately prior to a memorial service to tell them that they were all thinking about them.

Bereavement and the curriculum

Some LEAs have a topic on bereavement on their Agreed Syllabus on RE and some secondary schools have a unit on the subject in their PSHE. Circle time in primary school and form time in secondary school is also a good opportunity to discuss death, but I should definitely not use it if a pupil in the room had a recent death in the family. Of course, these only deal with the subject in theory. It is how you cope in practice which matters.

29 Private tutoring

The comforting news

Private tutoring is the easiest form of teaching known to mankind. If you have become accustomed to classes of up to 35 heterogeneous clients with widely varying levels of ability, good breeding and willingness to learn, finding that you can earn extra cash by teaching only one or two who are interested in learning and whose parents give absolute backing, is like a cold drink in the desert.

There is no hassle over discipline. You can concentrate on giving the child your full attention undisturbed by a long list of intrusions, so you can achieve a high level of progress quickly. It is lovely to hear the parents say how much they appreciate your achieving so much more than his class teacher, though irritating if you're the class teacher, and a parent tells you how much more progress the child is making with his private tutor than stuck in your class of 35. If you find yourself in the latter position, say 'I'm sure s/he does. All teachers get more progress with their private pupils than they do with their class. I've always achieved a higher standard with my private pupils'.

If the parent persists, reply with some of the following statistics:

- The school days lasts five hours, or 300 minutes.
- In a class of 30, each child receives the equivalent of ten minutes of individual attention per day, or 50 minutes per week – less than he gets in an hour of private tuition (primary).
- Their son/daughter has six lessons of 40 minutes each, or 240 minutes of French teaching per week.
- In a class of 30, each pupil receives the equivalent of eight minutes of individual attention per week (secondary).

Point out that there are probably no interruptions in an hour of tuition and a tutor can move the lesson on at the rate which suits the pupil, not the main body of the class.

As a private tutor, you're not bound by rules, which forbid schools to exclude pupils for wrecking the quality of education for the rest of the class, or cheekily answering you back. In the unlikely event of a pupil giving you bother, you can stop tutoring them any time you want.

A few precautions

Attractive as it sounds, I have only met one teacher who was so successful that he gave up his job and tutored full-time. It doesn't bring in enough money for a comfortable lifestyle, and any teachers who try it long term must sort out a private pension, otherwise they'll be doing it for the rest of their lives.

Also, beware the tax man. It is important to budget for an annual payment to Inland Revenue and put your tax form in on time to avoid paying a penalty. Remember to keep a record of any expenses, for example fares, you've incurred to set these off against income, for tax purposes.

Realistically, tutoring is best for providing some extra income; ideal for teachers who work part-time; or are at home looking after children or relatives; or are retired and not as a main salary.

Where to find your tutees

The only difficulty is in finding the first pupils because once you've started, parents are usually so pleased their child is improving, they tell their friends and so you can have a steady stream carrying on for years. The best way to acquire pupils is by word of mouth. Ask around and you can usually find someone who knows someone who wants a tutor. Advertising in the local rag, shop 'nosy board' or library often works.

What do you charge?

Some teachers are not sure what to charge. One guide is to telephone a local tutoring agency and ask how much they charge for primary and secondary. You may have to pretend to be a parent looking for a tutor as they're not likely to want to help the opposition. Whatever they tell you, add on 25–50 per cent, depending on the client's ability to pay. Some unions give a guideline, so it's worth a phone call to find out.

Working for an agency is the worst way to find pupils. They set their rate so low and take about one quarter of your earnings. Then it's difficult for you to charge a proper rate because when parents recommend you, they also tell them the price.

Setting the terms

When you find a pupil, explain your terms to the parents and give it to them in writing. Some tutors write up a simple contract and ask the parents to sign it. As with any profession, tell them that if they cancel the lesson with less than one or two day's notice, you still expect to be paid for it. This saves you a lot of inconvenience, as some parents make a habit of it. You can soften the blow by telling them that if you, yourself, cancel within the same period of notice, you will give them the next lesson free. No one can argue with that.

If parents start regularly cancelling the lesson, tell them you'll only continue on the basis that they pay for each lesson a week in advance and the payment is not returnable if they cancel. Likewise, if they never have cash with them and want to pay in arrears. If they refuse, you might as well discontinue the lessons. It's not worth the hassle.

They might want to bring the child along to meet you first. This seems reasonable, but sometimes parents ask for a free trial lesson to see if their child likes you. I would agree to the trial lesson, but not for free.

If parents regularly inconvenience you by picking their pupils up late, start charging extra for childminding. A friend of mine did so and the parent arrived promptly after that.

If you have to spend a lot of time outside the lesson marking their work, for example essays and examination papers, charge half the hourly rate for that, full rate if it's A-level or AS-level.

It is better not to go to a pupil's house unless it's very convenient. Even if you can charge for travelling, you waste a lot of time and it reduces your hourly rate. One might make an exception to this rule if the pupil or parent were disabled.

Sometimes parents try to persuade you to reduce your price after you have agreed it. Always say no, otherwise the word will go round and you'll have them all trying it. If they say they will go elsewhere, still say no, they are probably bluffing.

Protect yourself again

Some parents are afraid to leave their child in the home of a tutor who is unknown to them in case they harm the child, and in recent years, teachers' unions and headteachers have advised teachers never to be alone with pupils in case they make an accusation of abuse. The same could apply to private tutors. Again, statistically, men are more vulnerable to accusations of abuse than women teachers. It is better to tutor pupils in pairs if you do not know the family. Tutors, particularly men, might feel more comfortable with a parent staying in the room during the lesson, for the first few sessions at least.

Only a small number of the private tutors I've known have encountered difficulties, most pupils and parents are so cooperative and appreciative that the job is usually a pleasure.

30 Advice for overseas teachers in UK schools

Some parts of the UK are short of teachers and some schools in inner cities are desperately short. Every year thousands of teachers from Australia, New Zealand, Africa, Asia, Canada and the US come to the UK. They're welcomed with open arms by the distraught headteachers who are struggling to survive with a skeleton staff or high turnovers of supply teachers from agencies which drain school budgets.

I have worked with many overseas teachers over the years and have usually found them able, conscientious and well organized. South Africa, Australia and New Zealand in particular have plenty of teachers and so their standard of training and examination is high. They are accustomed to stable, well-organized schools, where they have a reasonable amount of freedom in how they implement the curriculum and the teachers' word is still, usually, the law of the classroom. Many have told me that coming to British inner cities was a severe shock to their systems.

Many southern hemisphere teachers end up in schools which are in Special Measures or Fresh Start schools, because these are the ones which are in most dire need of staff and also the ones which UK teachers find least attractive.

Watch out for the term 'Special Measures'. It means that the school has failed its Ofsted inspection and has been given a list of issues to put right. 'Fresh Start' means that the school was closed down after failure and reopened with a new name, uniform, head and probably deputy as well. Fresh Start schools have a year to get their act together and then they have a two-day HMI inspection every term until they are deemed satisfactory, usually after an Ofsted inspection.

Both schools have lots of problems, usually of discipline, staff and pupil morale and implementation of the curriculum.

So why do teachers come to the UK?

The UK is an attractive destination for overseas English-speaking teachers because there's no language barrier and they can easily find jobs. Some have told me that they can save enough to go travelling on the continent during the holidays. South Africans have told me they can save enough for the deposit on a house when they return home because their own property prices are so much cheaper than ours.

So what are the difficulties and how does the overseas teacher cope?

A variety of southern hemisphere teachers have told me the main issues which have caused them difficulties.

New climate, new environment

Southern hemisphere teachers find the British climate difficult. Accustomed to sunshine for long months of the year, they find they're severely limited to indoor activities only and this gives them a feeling of being housebound. Also the grey skies and short hours of daylight in winter has a depressing effect on them.

In large cities finding one's way to work is sometimes difficult on public transport. One teacher told me she felt as if she'd already done a day's work by the time she arrived at school. It is worth investing in the largest scale, best quality, colour A–Z or street finder. The clerk in the agency will give you directions on how to find your school, but not necessarily the most convenient. If your route is awkward, ask in the staffroom, there's usually someone who can tell you the simplest route.

It can be difficult to adjust to the lack of space in the city schools. Sparsely populated countries like Australia and New Zealand have large playing areas with wide expanses of grass both inside and outside the school environment. Some overseas teachers tell me that the small tarmacadam city playgrounds, often without a green area, make them feel claustrophobic, and they believe it's the cause of some of the conflict among the pupils.

Money

Often money is a problem because when teachers convert their savings into sterling, they find it does not buy as much as in their native country, putting pressure on them to grab a job fast.

Some have found the problem that they could not get a bank account because they had no permanent address, and could not get accommodation because they had no bank account. Some only managed to save themselves by finding a compatriot who allowed them to sleep in their living room and use their address until they earned some money.

Before you leave your home country, go to your bank and find the name of its sister bank in the UK and ask for a transfer, so that when you arrive you already have a bank account. If your bank doesn't have a sister bank in the UK, try other banks until you find one. Transfer as much money as you can before you arrive because our accommodation prices are high.

Work permits

It is worth trying to sort out a Residents' Work Permit before you leave home. When you arrive, some schools will not want to be bothered applying for one for you. It will depend on how eager they are to employ you, and remember the more desirable the school, the easier it will be for them to find a teacher locally.

Accommodation

Accommodation can be a problem in some areas of the country. Overseas teachers tell me there's a wide range of standards of accommodation available and at similar prices. So it's wise to look at several before making a decision. It is usually cheaper and more comfortable for two couples, or four single people, to find a larger property and share. Also the prices are often negotiable. Many landlords ask for more than they expect to get in rent.

At the time of writing, accommodation can also be found through the website www.gumtree.com so that can be fixed before you leave home. However, you may feel you would rather see a property first before you commit yourself to it. At the time of writing, you can advertise for accommodation on this website free of charge.

Teachers who arrived with nowhere to stay found accommodation through agencies and advertisements on shop 'nosy boards'.

Unfortunately, this can take time so it's important to bring money to pay for accommodation in a hostel or guest house until you organize something more stable.

There are some private schools, and even a small number of state schools, who can give you rented accommodation with the job. If they can it will say so in the advertisement.

Finding a job

Some heads can be so short of teachers they'll even interview overseas candidates over the phone, before they leave home. This can be set up for you by a supply teaching agency. It is great to be able to organize a job this way but be aware that if you do, the school will be very challenging. That is why the head cannot find a teacher at home.

It is easy to find a job in most city areas of the UK, although this is not the case in some country areas. Some teachers email teaching agencies to give them all their details before they leave their home country and this speeds up the process when they arrive in the UK. When you arrive, if you have no job to start with, there are lots of agencies advertising in the *Times Educational Supplement*.

In the first instance, try to find a school with fewer problems. You can do this by starting off with an agency. If you are in another city, telephone the London office and they'll give you the number of their office closest to you. If you are in an area where there are no agencies, find the address of the LEA from the phonebook and apply to join their list of supply teachers. If they say they have no supply list ask them to fax/email/post you a list of vacancies.

You can start by doing day to day work so that if you do find yourself in a problematical school you only have to put up with it for a day or two. If you find a fairly civilized school, you can start establishing a relationship with the head or head of department in case a job comes up. Heads like to employ people they know and have seen in action. See Chapter 18, 'Supply teaching', for further advice.

The largest single factor affecting the quality of life in a school is the head. I have known competent heads to lift failing schools out of the gutter and weak ones to send efficient schools into the gutter. Look for one with a strong head, who is competent at managing both people and the curriculum. This could take some time, so be patient and resist the temptation to accept the first contract you're offered, unless of course you are in an area where it is difficult to find a job.

If you can get into a private school, life is easier. You have smaller classes and the pupils do not present so many behavioural difficulties. There are more specialist teachers for music, art, PE and ICT, etc. so you get much more non-contact time to plan lessons and mark work. You may of course have to cope with pushy, ambitious parents but this is usually easier than disaffected pupils.

Most disconcerting of all is that the UK government doesn't always recognize overseas qualifications. This is particularly infuriating as some schools would fall apart without their overseas teachers and yet they can pay them less than the DfES rate. When you've taken a permanent or semi-permanent contract, the next thing you might want to sort out is Qualified Teacher Status if you don't already have it, in order to raise your own status and salary if you intend staying more than a year.

If you have a degree it can be sorted out fairly quickly within a term or two. If you trained in the 1960s or 1970s and only have a Teachers' Certificate or Diploma, then it's a lengthy process to upgrade your qualification. This seems unfair because there are many home-grown British teachers who trained in the 1970s and don't have degrees. Once you've got Qualified Teacher Status you can have your salary raised to the proper level. Remember, if you don't ask for it you won't get it.

Next you can apply for an incentive allowance and bump your salary up another thousand or two. If you've reached point M6 on the main pay scale and have been in the country for three years, start thinking about applying for the upper pay spine. Ask the head about it, and persevere.

If you're desperate to get a permanent job quickly, you can easily get one in a Fresh Start school or one in Special Measures. If you do, don't be afraid to negotiate your salary. Heads in these schools are often desperate for staff and don't receive so many applications from home-grown teachers.

When they offer you a job, say, 'It depends on the terms'. If your qualification is not automatically recognized, and the head offers you less than the going rate, say, 'That's not enough, I would be better off in a private school or one that isn't going to be inspected every term, for that amount'. Remember, these heads are desperate for good teachers. They need you more than you need them, so be brave. If they want you, they'll probably add on another thousand or two.

Pupils

Overseas teachers have told me the first difficulty is that the pupils have very different attitudes in some inner-city areas. Teachers who are accustomed to fairly innocent pupils, who want to learn, respect adults and even accept a smack from them, are shocked by the attitude of the 'sophisticated' city child who has been 'brought up on a diet of TV, their rights and talk about sex'.

Also, they say that teachers are not treated as professionals, as their judgement is frequently challenged by the press, and children, often trained by their parents, treat teachers with disrespect. It is a blow to discover that respect cannot be taken for granted: it has to be earned. But it can be earned if you strike up a rapport with the parents of a difficult child. Before you send for a parent whom you haven't met, always ask a senior member of staff first, in case the parent is antagonistic or even violent. Some schools have a list of parents with whom teachers do not speak alone, or at all in some cases.

If you have pupils with negative attitudes it's difficult, though very important, to remember that all pupils have a need to be loved and shown care, even if they alternately exhibit a mixture of scorn and indifference to you and their education. After they have worn you out by challenging everything you have said and tried to undermine your authority at every point, it's important to come in the next day without rancour. When they begin to show the first signs of compliance, shower them with praise.

Behind the facade of aggression there's usually a young person who is desperate for affection and appreciation and an overwhelming need to be valued. This, of course, is more easily said than done, and often takes at least half a term to achieve, so try not to become disheartened if improvement does not come quickly.

Overseas teachers sometimes complain that pupils don't have enough games lessons which leaves them with surplus energy and without the skills of organizing themselves to play games independently. This leads to fighting through lack of the skills of playing cooperatively. Pupils then come into the classroom with feelings of distress or anger instead of being refreshed, leaving them less receptive to learning.

Some teachers resolve this by the use of circle time in the primary school (or form time in the secondary school). The pupils and teacher sit in a circle and discuss the issue which is causing grief and make suggestions about how to solve the problems, for example bullying in the playground. Usually pupils pass a little object – I use a soft toy – around the circle and pupils can only speak when they've the toy in their hand. If they don't want to speak, they say 'Pass' and give the toy to the next pupil. Ignore any pupils who speak out of turn, and at the end ask the pupils who didn't speak if they would like the opportunity to do so. It often works by making pupils stop and think about their own behaviour and see a better way of coping with conflict.

Even if not entirely successful, it often diffuses anger and helps pupils to settle down to work. So it can be time well spent even if it uses up 15 minutes of your lesson time.

One teacher told me that in his own country he never worried about which class he would be given the following year, whereas some UK teachers frequently worry about being given a hell-raiser class next. If you intend to return to your (primary) school after the summer holidays, it's wise to look around the school in June, decide which class you would like and ask the head if you can have it the following year. It sometimes works.

New Zealanders who are used to only one or two cultures in the classroom have told me they had to cope with a period of adjustment to having a wide variety of races, religions, native languages and levels of knowledge of English. Some have even told me that it took several days to learn to pronounce all the names on the register correctly.

You can be faced with a class with at least half of whom speak English as their second or third language, and several pupils who speak very little English at all. This can be a daunting situation if you're not used to dealing with it. Try not to think of this as a problem because it frequently isn't.

Pupils with English as an additional language (EAL) usually pick the language up quickly, especially if they've been to school in their own country, and they're normally eager to learn it. We all like to know what everyone is talking about! If they are refugees from a country with sparse educational provision, they may well be unaccustomed to having something interesting to do and be eager to take part in practical lessons where language is not such a barrier.

If pupils cannot speak much English, try to put them beside a child who speaks the same native tongue and English as well, and ask him or her to translate. This means you must be prepared to tolerate them talking quietly during lesson.

The school may have some dual text books in the pupil's native language. This is a great help both in making the pupils feel at home and in helping them to pick up English as they can read in their own language first and compare the two texts to match up the words. If the school has not got a supply of dual text books you can always borrow some from the LEA's resource library.

Most multicultural schools have a teacher designated to help and advise so don't be afraid to ask for help. No one will blame you for not having much experience and will be pleased that you're conscientious enough to want to get it right.

Some teachers have told me that they thought the pupils would find them interesting because they were from abroad, and would like to know about their country and why they spoke with a different accent. This turned out to be laughable since many classes are accustomed to having a stream of overseas teachers and some have had a different class teacher, and sometimes two, every term for years. In fact some classes have lost interest in teachers since they've worked out that they won't be around for long.

If you are staying in the school for the year, it can be difficult to gain the pupils' trust and respect, and perseverance is the only answer. It improves after the first holiday when they see you've actually come back.

Some overseas teachers have difficulty in communicating with pupils. If they cannot understand your accent, they'll not even try to listen to you. You will have to speak more slowly and tone down your accent. If you use a lot of the idiomatic language of your own country, the pupils will look at you as if you're mad, and you'll soon learn which expressions not to use.

If you use a lot of different vowel sounds and have to teach the pupils to read with phonics, you absolutely must adjust to using the same sounds as the pupils. Sometimes teachers object to this, believing it is undervaluing their own culture, but it isn't. I found myself in this predicament in my first year when I struggled to communicate with pupils in the East End of London with my strong Irish accent. Listening carefully to their speech, while slowing down and modifying my own, meant the difference in being understood or ignored by pupils.

Staff

Supply teachers complain that when working in some schools for a few days, or less, even teachers show them little regard, treating them with total indifference. In some schools supply teachers are ignored for days and teachers don't even look them in the eye. This probably happens because those schools have so many supplies, and teachers are so preoccupied with their own difficulties that they can't work up the energy to bother with someone who is here today and gone tomorrow. If this happens to you, take the initiative and begin a conversation in the staffroom. British teachers are normally friendly, but you may need to put the effort in to form a friendly working relationship.

The system

Many of the overseas teachers of my acquaintance dislike the UK system for a variety of reasons.

Overseas teachers (and many British teachers) say that our system is based on the three Ts – targets, tests and tables. The thematic approach, whereby primary pupils explore a topic of interest, is still used in some overseas countries, New Zealand for example, but in the UK it has given way to a subject-based curriculum and an obsession with making sure that each child achieves the appropriate level for their age group in the wretched annual tests. This 'squashes the curriculum', adds pressure and takes the pleasure out of what ought to be an enjoyable and creative job. If you find it impossible to fulfil all the objectives of every lesson, it is best to prioritize and make sure you cover all of the English, maths and science, as these are tested by the SATs and QCA tests.

Overseas teachers are often amazed that the National Curriculum is foisted onto every child in the country, regardless of whether they are new to the UK, speak little English and live in one room in sleazy accommodation for the homeless, or have had a cultured background in the country or wealthy suburbia. Teachers don't legally have the discretion to withdraw pupils from it if they don't believe it fulfils their needs.

One option is to ask the special needs teacher or EAL teacher to prepare simplified versions of each lesson for the pupils they're supporting. This works in many occasions but if the history or geography lesson is completely beyond the pupil, don't bang your head against the wall trying to achieve the impossible, ask your support teacher or classroom assistant to do some basic maths or English with the pupils instead, and be prepared to stand up to anyone who objects.

Use expressions like, 'I am doing what best fulfils the pupils' immediate needs. I am not depriving the child of his/her right to the geography National Curriculum. I am merely postponing it until s/he can read well enough to enjoy the benefit of the Foundation curriculum'. If you can show that the child is benefiting from whatever s/he is given, heads and senior staff will usually accept that.

Nonetheless, it's wiser not to sit in the staffroom complaining about the inappropriateness of the National Curriculum for all of your English as a second or third language learners. That draws attention to the fact that you're not teaching it all to them and can create waves. It's always best to let the senior staff find out first, and then start justifying your decisions.

The National Curriculum is prescribed in detail and the lack of freedom to teach in your own way is very daunting. Overseas teachers, unaccustomed to having to present such copious, minutely detailed plans, say that the planning actually distracts them from the task of teaching, and so it's counter-productive. Also, having to spend so much time on them is tiring and so you give a less vigorous and enthusiastic performance in the classroom.

I found the most time-economic way of presenting plans is to do them on the computer. Most schools can give you a floppy disk with a skeleton of their lesson format. Once you've put on the first week's plan, the next can be superimposed on it. Some items will be the same each week so you can just change the details. If you keep all your plans and worksheets in well-organized folders, and take copies of them on to your next school, whether you're allowed to or not, you avoid the frustration of having to re-invent it all.

Also, it's best to prepare only a week in advance, so that if it doesn't work out as planned you will have fewer changes to make.

In primary schools the rigid three-part lessons for literacy and numeracy hours feel like a straitjacket and sometimes the plans written a week in advance don't always go as expected, and you want to change the pace to suit the pupils' ability to grasp each concept. I was once in a borough where advisory teachers went around schools and checked that the work in the pupils' books matched the daily plan. Teachers who were a day or two out, got a flea in their ear.

If this happens to you, be prepared to stand up for yourself. Point out that it's counter-productive, especially in maths, to force pupils on to the next stage before they've mastered the present one. Use expressions like, 'A plan is a servant, not a master,' and 'Pupils' needs are far more important than paper!' or 'It is impossible to judge exactly what each individual pupil can achieve in each lesson. If I judge three-quarters of it correctly, I think I am doing well'. Don't be afraid of an argument. Even if you annoy them, they will realize you're not a soft touch and think twice about hassling you the next time.

When you get used to what the pupils can do, it's easier to judge how much you can achieve in each lesson. In the beginning you may find it easier to put less on paper, although you may have more work prepared, then if you achieve what is written down it looks satisfactory and anything extra is a bonus. No one gets it all right in the beginning, so don't despair or let anyone make you feel you're underachieving.

In some schools there's a large amount of regimentation. Some heads want to direct much of the classroom organization, even to the extent of dictating what is pinned on the classroom display boards. This is not an exaggeration. I have known two heads who did so. Although this might aid the teacher who wants guidance, it stifles the creativity of the enthusiastic teacher with an inventive mind. I would fall in with the head's wishes to start with. After you're established in the school, you'll be able to exercise a bit of your own creativity.

Some overseas teachers complain that the pupils are heavily pressurized in academic subjects and the timetable doesn't leave pupils much time for fun activities like art, PE, games, cooking and the opportunity to enjoy the fun of being a child.

There is copious detail in the core curriculum – English, maths and science – and often it's impossible to do the job well because the butter is spread so thinly. Even the Foundation curriculum – history, geography, art, etc. is heavily laden with clearly defined objectives, so there's constant pressure to fulfil each minute detail and never time to joke, relax and enjoy a lesson. I found it better to try to do less and do it well. If you're challenged by the postholder for not achieving all the objectives, say, 'I have done as many as is possible in the time allotted. If you want to persuade the head to allocate a higher number of hours to your subject I'm sure I'll achieve more'.

In the UK there's an enormous amount of monitoring and checking up on teachers. This is disconcerting to an outsider because it looks like a lack of trust, which of course it is. There is also a blame culture. (I think the polite word is 'accountability'.) The head and senior staff are constantly checking curriculum plans, monitoring performance and keeping notes to cover their backs in case the SATs, QCA, GCSE or A-level results are low and they're blamed for not spotting problems and doing something about it.

There is not much specialization in UK state primary schools so teachers have to teach nearly every subject and have very little non-contact time during the school day.

Resources are sometimes a problem. Some schools are well resourced and supply teachers are given the day's lessons by the head of department in secondary school, or year group coordinator, as soon as they arrive. In others they are left to flounder alone and I'm told it is always the worst schools with the most difficult pupils where the latter is the case. Carry with you a set of activities, which you have already tried out at college or your last school, which are enjoyable and adaptable for different ages.

Most overseas teachers I spoke to told me they had teething troubles in their first term. The keyword is 'persevere'. Most became accustomed to the new system and way of life and I've worked with quite a lot who were so successful in their schools that they decided to stay on for more years than they intended. Some gave up on the state system and found jobs in private schools which they enjoyed so much they prolonged their stay in the UK indefinitely.

31 If it all goes wrong, what else can a teacher do?

Sadly, the teaching profession has a high fall-out rate. Mediocre pay, an inadequate career structure, an ever-increasing paperload, much of which gives no job satisfaction, and the stress of disciplining ever-increasing numbers of pupils, who are beyond their parents' control: all these take their toll on the nation's supply of teachers.

Many teachers persevere for too long because they cannot find another bolt-hole. Some teachers who are desperate to escape from the classroom, but have a talent for administration, find refuge in applying for promotion to deputy headship or headship. Others are so disenchanted they leave the profession completely.

Joining the escape committee?

There is sometimes one of these committees in the staffroom. They become active at periods when teachers are at a low ebb, such as at the end of a long or stressful term, or before or during Ofsted. If you're seriously thinking that you're in the wrong job, don't do anything rash . . . yet. Stop and ask yourself, 'what is your main anxiety?' Is it:

- the teaching;
- the pupils;
- your colleagues;
- the head;
- the parents;
- the money;
- the paperwork;
- lack of job satisfaction;
- long hours;
- stress/you're losing your sanity?

Often it's a combination of two or more of these. Now ask yourself what you would most miss about teaching if you gave up. Is it:

- the holidays;
- the job security and steady income;
- the company;
- the interaction with pupils;
- job satisfaction?

Now make a list of what is important to you in order of priority. It might look like this:

1   Steady income.
2   Holidays to keep you sane.
3   Being treated with respect and fairness.
4   Being in control.
5   Job satisfaction.

Now you need to study the lists and weigh up whether you need:

- to move into another teaching job, if you like teaching but find your present post unsatisfactory;
- to try for promotion if you want more money, or less classroom work, or both;
- to teach part-time because you need the money while you sort out something less stressful for the rest of the week;
- to use your knowledge and skills to do a job related to teaching;
- leave teaching completely.

So what are the options?

Moving sideways
Many teachers love teaching, but hate the hassle of coping with stroppy kids and the mountains of paperwork.

Many have taken a sideways move into private schools after years in the state sector and found that their feeling of achievement and self-worth was restored. Private schools can pay the same, a little more or a little less. They don't always have the same pension scheme as the state sector so you have to check that out before you move.

All the teachers who I know who have done it, said the money was irrelevant to them. The improved working conditions of smaller classes, more highly motivated pupils, better resources and a few perks like nutritious, free meals made it well worth their while, even with the irritation of ambitious, over anxious parents.

I have known a variety of teachers who moved to adult education. They found teaching adults, who attended classes of their own freewill and choice, to be beneficial to their (the teachers') health and sense of job satisfaction. There isn't usually much financial benefit in moving into adult institutes, but the reduction in classroom stress can be a good enough reason for doing it.

Moving upwards

Others with degrees have gone back to university to become lecturers on teacher training courses and found it stimulating and rewarding. Some have returned to university to do Masters' degrees and then found jobs as advisory teachers, advisors or as college or university lecturers.

Some teachers have gone back to university to do Masters' degrees to become educationalist psychologists (EPs) and found no difficulty in adjusting to the rise in their income, the enhanced status and release from the daily pressure of full classes. Every LEA employs a team of EPs to visit schools to administer tests and assessments to diagnose pupils' learning and behavioural difficulties and advise teachers on how to manage their problems. They also assess pupils for entry into special schools and various types of educational units provided by the LEA.

I have worked with a variety of EPs and noticed that the ones who had a long experience of teaching gave the most practical advice and got the most respect from parents and teachers. You need sound communication skills for this job because you have to work with parents who may be unable to accept their children's difficulties, or who have learning and behavioural difficulties themselves.

However, in some authorities, EPs are over stretched and some have told me that being expected to cover a large number of schools can be stressful. One showed me his diary and it was packed solid with appointments.

Moving out of the country

Every year hundreds of teachers move abroad to teach in international schools, most of which want teachers who are fluent in English. Jobs of this type are advertised on the Internet and in the *Times Educational Supplement*. Often working in a system which is less pressurized, in a new environment and sunnier (or cooler) climate gives teachers a new lease on life.

International schools are a fairly safe option because they often pay more than the local state schools, so you can live comfortably while you enjoy the new experience. The working conditions are normally favourable and the school management are usually helpful in finding their teachers comfortable, affordable accommodation when they arrive. Some give teachers a resettlement allowance to help them settle in and feel welcome.

The experience looks impressive on your CV. Obviously this is only practical for the unattached or those whose partners are willing to accompany them. Having children is not an impediment because these schools often welcome the children of staff and there's usually a massive reduction in school fees for children of the staff. Every teacher who I know who has done it, recommended it.

At the moment this could be an attractive option for secondary teachers because many schools abroad teach the International Baccalaureate, which is likely to be adopted in the UK in the near future. In fact some schools are teaching it already. Any teacher who returns to the UK with recent experience of teaching it should have no difficulty in finding a post in a desirable school.

Voluntary Service Overseas (VSO) is still an option for the unattached. Details are available from www.vso.org.uk. Teachers who have done this have given me widely varying accounts of their experiences. It's best to ask a lot of questions about the type of school environment before you go as I have met some who found the working conditions poor, and not all found it a happy and healthy experience.

If you log in to the Internet and type 'voluntary services overseas' or 'teachers abroad' into a search engine, you'll find dozens of websites for short and long-term working trips abroad. I have no knowledge of these trips but if you're looking for a new challenge in a new environment, you may find one which is worth a try.

Moving to the periphery

Part-time

MARKING SKILLS   If you're used to marking books and find that errors of spelling, punctuation and grammar jump off the page, you can do a course in proof-reading and earn up to £20 an hour working at home, if you can get the work. This is useful for teachers with young children and others who want to work part-time and at home. You can learn proof-reading by correspondence course. Find details on the website www.chapterhousepublishing.com or telephone 0800 328 8396.

There are often advertisements in the *Writers' News* and *Writing Magazine*. Before you start, though, it's wise to make enquiries to find out how much work is available. You could ring up some publishers of books in your sphere of knowledge to find if they have vacancies for trained proof-readers.

Publishers also employ people for copy-editing and indexing which can also be done part-time, or freelance, and so it's convenient for people who have family commitments.

AQA and other examining bodies are always on the lookout for markers for SATs, GCSE, AS-levels and A-level papers. It's easier to get work marking English than Maths or Science, because the latter are easier to mark. Look on their website for details: www.aqa.org.uk. This can be a handy extra to earn about an extra £1,000 once a year.

INVIGILATING EXAMINATION SKILLS   This is another seasonal way to earn some extra cash. It's obviously much easier than teaching, and the students don't present any problems because they're engrossed in passing their examinations. You can approach schools directly, or telephone your LEA to ask if there are any vacancies.

COMMUNICATION SKILLS   Some who wanted to work part-time have found posts as communicators for the partially hearing. One teacher told me how she took a course in communication for the deaf and now accompanies students to lectures and takes notes for them. Afterwards she passes on the notes and explains any points which are unclear. Although not highly paid, this job offers enjoyment if the subject is interesting and job satisfaction when one's students are able to access a curriculum which was formerly closed to them.

Some communicators for the deaf and partially hearing have gone on to learn sign language and the most successful have become deaf interpreters for the Royal Shakespeare Company on their deaf evenings. This is a much prized and well-paid skill.

Full-time and part-time

CURRICULUM SKILLS   Have you got experience of developing teaching programmes? There are frequently advertisements in the *Times Educational Supplement* for teachers to develop courses.

PRESENTATIONAL SKILLS   Some teachers are not in favour of private education but can find work in the many tourist sites which have an education department. Museums, cathedrals and school journey centres employ teachers to organize activities for pupils on educational trips.

Pupils usually behave better on a day trip than they do in school and the novelty of being in a different environment often excites them so they forget to misbehave. Even if you do have the occasional difficult class, you don't go home feeling stressed about it because you'll probably never have to see them again.

If you prefer to work with adults, museums, stately homes, tourist sites, art galleries and conservation sites employ guides to lead visiting adult groups around buildings and sites. Although one occasionally has a difficult adult in the group, behaviour management is not a problem.

PHYSICAL EDUCATION SKILLS   Leisure centres, swimming pools, outdoor pursuits centres and school journey centres employ staff to supervise and train children and adults. Remember, people attend these places voluntarily and so you have a willing class. Even if pupils do misbehave on their weekly school trip to the swimming baths, you can exclude them from the lesson on safety grounds.

COMPUTER SKILLS   Are you competent with computers? LEAs need teachers to organize courses to train other teachers to make best use of them in schools. Are you competent with interactive whiteboards? Currently schools throughout the country are aiming to equip themselves with them and the companies who supply them need demonstrators to instruct teachers on how to use them. It's an attractive job – teaching fellow professionals who want to learn.

Some larger schools employ learning facilitators in ICT. Their job is to support the pupils' learning using computers. They assist teachers by finding programs to teach specific skills to pupils. They also surf the Internet to find resources and useful websites for teachers who don't have the time or technical skills to do it themselves.

They also encourage and guide technophobe teachers like me, who took a long time to get used to computers.

LIBRARY SKILLS   Most teachers like libraries. I know one teacher who successfully made the transfer to being a librarian by undertaking the training course and then found her stress levels diminish dramatically.

EDUCATIONALLY CREATIVE SKILLS   Television channels run educational programmes. Who better than teachers to employ to create them? Don't wait to see the posts advertised: ring up all the television companies who have educational programmes of the age group for which you've been trained, and ask if they have vacancies. If you have ideas for interesting programmes, ring up television companies and ask if they would like to see sample scripts.

Moving out of the profession

This option is probably only open to you if have something else lined up to do, you have more savings than most teachers or you have parents or a partner who can support you financially. Teachers do have transferable personal skills in addition to knowledge and understanding:

- keeping an audience interested with eye contact and voice intonation;
- explaining difficult concepts by breaking them into manageable parts;
- communicating ideas in a persuasive manner;
- establishing positive relationships and gaining the trust and respect of a wide range of people;

- presenting boring ideas and concepts creatively to make them interesting;
- taking a lot of cold facts and writing them up in an organized, attractive manner;
- taking in a large body of information quickly and using it effectively;
- acting skills – all teachers incorporate some play acting into their daily work and some are real comedians.

Now look at your professional skills:

- computer literacy;
- languages;
- pastoral care;
- communication;
- writing;
- performing arts;
- business;
- knowledge of your subject(s).

Can you combine your personal and professional skills to find yourself a niche?

Computer literacy
Are you competent with computers? I have known of teachers to take their ICT expertise into industry and increase their salary quickly.

Language skills
Have you got a language degree? I have known language graduates to work as translators in international firms at home and abroad. Also some publishers who produce books in two or more languages need translators and proof-readers to ensure that the translations are accurate.

Pastoral skills
Many teachers have a talent for pastoral care and organization. I know one who left to become a warden of a children's home.

Some colleges employ managers to live in their residential accommodation to supervise their international students and organize the catering and cleaning services. These jobs are not well paid but they do include free accommodation. You can find advertisements for them in the *TES*.

Communication skills

A teacher's main skill is the art of communication, an invaluable gift for a salesman. I have been advised by a personnel manager in industry, that teachers make successful sales people because they've the technique of putting their message across clearly and quickly. Teachers who are accustomed to keeping disinterested pupils on board are ideal. Insurance companies, financial investment companies, publishers and every manufacturing industry in the country can use disenchanted teachers to peddle their products.

Organizations like the National Trust employ people to recruit members. Teachers are ideal for this as they have the knack of making activities look appealing. I know one teacher who now enjoys a job with the National Trust, working in an attractive environment without the stress of teaching.

Writing skills

A small number of teachers have taken to writing to make money. This can be a long-term project, and there's no guarantee that you can make money at it, but it's worth a try if you have a flair for creative writing, or skill in expressing facts succinctly and in an interesting way.

I teach full-time and I'm writing this book in the evenings, weekends and holidays. Some teachers who have become successful writers have managed to support themselves by combining writing with two or three days per week of supply teaching. Many teachers have succeeded but even if you manage to earn money as a writer, it's not wise to give up the day job completely unless you win the Booker prize or Steven Spielberg rings up for the film rights of your novel!

For expert guidance try the Writers' Bureau, Sevendale House, 7 Dale Street, Manchester, M1 1JB; Tel: 0161 228 2362 or fax: 0161 228 3533 or website: www.writersbureau.com. They run a successful correspondence course which has helped many writers establish themselves.

Another sound investment is to subscribe to the *Writers' News* and the *Writing Magazine*. For under £50 per annum you receive two magazines per month packed with advice from the experts, competitions, writers courses and advertisements for self-publishers. They have helped many writers like me get started. You can telephone their subscription department 01778 392 482 or email subscription@warnersgroup.co.uk; website: www.writersnews. co.uk. You can buy the *Writing Magazine* in WH Smith's.

If you have a talent for writing short stories, you could study a magazine which produces the type of story you like writing and try sending them one. Write to the publisher and ask for their guidelines first, and then read a few copies of the magazine before you send in a story, because they all have a specific style and won't consider anything which doesn't comply. This is a very difficult market to break into and it's not lucrative, but worth a try if you enjoy reading and writing short stories.

Are you a teacher with a talent for creating resources like maths games for children? Are you a special needs teacher who can never find suitable books with an interest level to match your pupils' reading level? Some publishing houses are on the look-out for materials produced by serving teachers. Try Educational Printing Services Limited, website: www.eprint.co.uk.

Look at the name of the publisher of any books or materials similar to what you can produce and then look at their website. Somewhere on it you'll find a format of the book proposals or educational materials they like to receive. Ring them up and ask if they're interested in your ideas. You have a better chance of being accepted if you type up your proposal to match their format exactly.

Everything sent to a publisher must be in mint condition, accompanied by your CV and a letter explaining why your work is useful and to whom. You have to enclose a stamped, self-addressed envelope if you want it returned.

Copywriting is a lucrative form of writing. A copywriter is employed by companies, organizations, local government departments, marketing and advertising agencies to write up information for publication, for example in brochures. Have you got the skill of presenting cold facts in a manner which is interesting and appealing to the reader? Some teachers start by making leaflets for local businesses, and then approaching the owners to try to interest them in offering work.

Do you have specialized knowledge? Others look at their own specialist knowledge and approach companies and magazines with articles they've written.

Freelance Copywriting by Diana Wimbs (1999), a successful freelance copywriter, gives tips on the trade.

Performing arts skills

Can you play a musical instrument? I knew a music teacher who got a job in an orchestra and others who have played in gigs to earn extra cash. It seems best to work part-time until you get established before giving up the day job.

Similarly, some have gone into acting, although occasionally they did have to resort to supply teaching during the 'rest' periods.

Business skills

In London, some teachers have found a way to make a living by setting up agencies for supply teachers. I know one overseas teacher who returned to New Zealand and ran an agency to recruit teachers for the UK.

Knowledge of your subject

Some teachers are very knowledgable about their subject but don't necessarily want to be writers. Some teachers have talent for recognizing a book which would sell well.

Publishers employ commissioning editors to advise their companies on which books to publish, and then work with authors to get the books written. If you know your subject thoroughly, and can can judge which books would be useful, and then sell well, for your area of education, you could try to get a job with an educational publisher. It is, however, very difficult to get a job in commissioning and it may be necessary to start in some other area of publishing first, usually as an editorial assistant.

Most publishing houses are in London and Oxford but there's a scattering of publishers throughout the country.

32 The last word

'IF' (with apologies to Rudyard Kipling)

If you can keep your cool when all around are losing theirs
And blaming it on the headmaster.
If you can cope with lost kids on school trips, impromptu class
   assemblies
And all-in fights, without disaster.

If you can face unpopularity and criticism
In order to put the blooming kids first.
If you can defend your colleagues when they're wrong,
Knowing you will probably come out worst.

If you can laugh and start again
When all your work and efforts are brought to nought.
If you can keep kids on your side
When they know you've not prepared your lessons as you ought.

If you can patiently explain the simplest principle
Again and again and again and again.
If you can sanction and reprimand and at the end of the day
Still be regarded as a friend.

If you can persuade the kids to take SATs seriously
Though you know they're just a farce.
If you can avoid telling the head
To shove his targets up his arse.

If you can encourage and keep on board the child who always
    fails
No matter how hard he tries.
If you can make them take pride in their place in the league tables,
Knowing they're just a Government PR exercise.

If you can care about Ofsted enough to pass,
But not so much as to sink into depression.
If you can cope with disappointment and failure
Several times in swift succession.

If you can make your point and stand firm,
In the face of opposition, without aggression.
You will last until you're pensioned off, and what's much more,
You will survive the teaching profession.

                                                    H. A. Bennett

Appendix

Abbreviations

A-levels	Advanced Levels
AS-levels	Advanced Subsidiary
AST	Advanced Skills Teacher
ATL	Association of Teachers and Lecturers
AUT	Association of University Teachers
AQA	Assessment and Qualifications Alliance
CRE	Commission for Racial Equality
CV	Curriculum Vitae
DfES	Department for Education and Skills
EAL	English as an Additional Language
EIS	Educational Institute of Scotland
EP	Educational Psychologist
EMAG	Ethnic Minority Achievement Grant
GCSE	General Certificate of Secondary Education
GTTP	Graduate Teacher Training Programme
HMI	Her Majesty's Inspectorate
ICT	Information and Communications Technology
INTO	Irish National Teachers' Organisation
Inset	In-service education of teachers
IT	Information Technology
KS	Key Stage
LEA	Local Education Authority
MA	Master of Arts
NASUWT	National Association of Schoolmasters and Union of Women Teachers
NAHT	National Association of Head Teachers
NC	National Curriculum
NFER	National Foundation for Educational Research
NOF	New Opportunities Funding (for computer training)
NQT	Newly qualified teacher
NUT	National Union of Teachers

Ofsted	Office for Standards in Education
PAT	Professional Association of Teachers
PE	Physical Education
PGCE	Post-Graduate Certificate in Education
PSHE	Personal, Social and Health Education
RE	Religious Education
SACRE	Standing Advisory Committee for Religious Education
SAT	Standardized Assessment Tests
SEN	Special Educational Needs
SENCO	Special Educational Needs Coordinator
SHA	Secondary Heads Association
SSTA	Scottish Secondary Teachers' Association
TES	*Times Educational Supplement*
QCA	Qualifications and Curriculum Authority
QTS	Qualified Teacher Status
UTU	Ulster Teachers' Union
VSO	Voluntary Service Overseas

Teachers' unions and associations

Association of Teachers and Lecturers (ATL) (171,000 members)
7 Northumberland Street, London, WC2N 5RD.
Tel: 020 7930 6441
Fax: 020 7930 1359
Email: info@atl.org.uk
Website: www.atl.org.uk

Association of University Teachers (AUT) (31,000 members)
Egmont House, 25–31 Tavistock Place, London, WC1H 9UT.
Tel: 020 7670 9700
Fax: 020 7670 9799
Email: hq@aut.org.uk
Website: www.aut.org.uk

Educational Institute of Scotland (EIS) (50,000 members)
46 Moray Place, Edinburgh, EH3 6BH.
Tel: 0131 225 6244
Fax: 0131 220 3151
Email: enquiries@eis.org.uk
Website: www.eis.org.uk

Irish National Teachers' Organisation (INTO) (6,000 members)
23 College Gardens, Belfast, BT9 6BS.
Tel: 028 9038 1455
Fax: 028 9066 2803
Email: info@ni.ie
Website: www.into.ie

Irish National Teachers' Organisation (INTO) in the Republic of Ireland
(31,000 members)
35 Parnell Square, Dublin 1
Tel: +353 1 804 7700
Fax: +353 1 872 2462
Email: info@into.ie
Website: www.into.ie

National Association of Head Teachers (NAHT) (41,000 members)
1 Heath Square, Boltro Road, Haywards Heath, W. Sussex, RH16 1BL.
Tel: 01444 472 472/472 411
Fax: 01444 472 473
Email: info@naht.org.uk
Website: www.naht.org.uk

National Association of Schoolmasters and Union of Women Teachers
(NASUWT) (234,000 members)
Hillscourt Education Centre, Rose Hill, Rednal, Birmingham, BS4 8RS.
Tel: 0121 453 6150
Fax: 0121 457 6208/6209
Email: membership@mail.nasuwt.org.uk
nasuwt@mail.nassuwt.org.uk
Website: www.teachersunion.org.uk

NASUWT in Scotland
6 Waterloo Place, Edinburgh, EH1 3BG.
Tel: 0131 523 1110
Fax: 0131 523 1119
Email: rc-scotland@mail.nasuwt.org.uk
Website: www.teachersunion.org.uk

NASUWT in Wales
NASUWT Cymru, Greenwood Close, Cardiff Gate Business Park,
Cardiff, CF23 8RD.
Tel: 029 2054 6080
Fax: 029 2054 6089
Email: rc-wales-cymru@mail.nasuwt.org.uk
Website: www.teachersunion.org.uk/cymru

National Association of Teachers in Further and Higher Education
(NATFHE) (71,000 members)
27 Britannia Street, London, WC1X 9JP.
Tel: 020 7837 3636
Fax: 020 7837 4403
Minicom: 020 7278 0470
Email: hq@natfhe.org.uk
Website: www.natfhe.org.uk

National Union of Teachers (NUT) (248,000 members)
Hamilton House, Mabledon Place, London, WC1H 9BD.
Tel: 020 7380 4747
Fax: 020 7387 8458
Membership hotline 0845 300 1669
Website: www.teachers.org.uk

Professional Association of Teachers (PAT) (43,000 members; for
teachers in England and Wales)
2 St James' Court, Friar Gate, Derby, DE1 1BT.
Tel: 01332 372 337
Fax: 01332 290 310
Email: hq@pat.org.uk
Website: www.pat.org.uk

Professional Association of Teachers in Scotland (for teachers in Scotland
and N. Ireland)
1–3 Colne Street, Edinburgh, EH3 6AA.
Tel: 0131 220 8241
Fax: 0131 220 8350
Email: scotland@pat.org.uk
Website: www.pat.org.uk

Scottish Secondary Teachers' Association (SSTA) (7,000 members)
15 Dundas Street, Edinburgh, EH3 6QG.
Tel: 0131 556 5919
Fax: 0131 556 1419
Email: info@ssta.org.uk
Website: www.ssta.org.uk

Secondary Heads' Association (SHA) (9,000 members)
130 Regent Road, Leicester, LE1 7PG.
Tel: 0116 299 1122
Fax: 0116 299 1123
Email: info@sha.org.uk
Website: www.sha.org.uk

Ulster Teachers Union (UTU) (7,000 members)
94 Malone Road, Belfast, BT9 5HP.
Tel: 028 9066 2216
Fax: 028 9068 3296
Email: office@utu.edu
Website: www.utu.edu

Teaching agencies

Associated Education
Tel: 01643 707 085
Email: kerryevans@btconnect.org
Somerset and Devon

Career Teachers
Tel: 020 7382 4270; 0845 880 0950
Email: info@careerteachers.co.uk
London

Capita Education Resourcing
Tel: 0800 731 6871 Primary
Tel: 0800 731 6872 Secondary
Tel: 0800 731 6873 SEN
Tel: 0800 316 1332 Further Education
Email: ers@capita.co.uk
Branches nationwide

Celsian:education
Tel: 0845 606 0676
Email: enquiries@celsiangroup.co.uk
Branches nationwide

Class Act Teaching Services
Tel: 0800 028 6196
Email: classact@teachingservices.fsnet.co.uk
Hertfordshire, Oxfordshire, Warwickshire, Yorkshire

Concorde Teaching Bank
Tel: 01872 262 033
Email: concordeteachingbank@cornwall.ac.uk
Cornwall and Isles of Scilly

Cover Teachers
Tel: 0117 973 5695
Email: enquiries@coverteachers.co.uk
S.W. England

Education Recruitment Network
Tel: 01633 223 747
Email: erninfo@aol.com
Wales, S. England and Jersey

Hays Education
Tel: 0800 716 026
Email: enquiries@hays-education.com
England and Wales

Key Stage Teacher Supply
Tel: 01254 298 616
Email: info@keystagesupply.co.uk
E. Lancashire; M65 corridor

ITN Teachers
Tel: 020 7246 4777
Email: admin@itnteachers.com
London and home counties

Link Education
Tel: 0845 130 4586
Email: linkeducation@btconnect.com
Kent, Essex, Bexley, Bromley

Long-term Teachers
Tel: 0845 130 6149
Email: info@longtermteachers.com
England

Masterlock Recruitment
Tel: 0117 915 4567 West Country
Tel: 020 7229 6699
Email: info@masterlock.co.uk
London and Home counties

Mark Education
Tel: 01534 62112
Email: info@markeducation.co.uk
England and Wales

Marverose
Tel: 0870 429 4845
Email: marveroseteachers@safe-mail.net
S.E. England and abroad

Protocol Teachers
Tel: 020 8515 6655; 0845 450 9450
Email: info@protocolteachers.com
Text: 81025 'teach', name and postcode
Branches nationwide

Quality Teacher Recruitment
Tel: 0800 783 7405
Email: qtr@supplyteaching.com
Norfolk

Quay Education Services
Tel: 020 7535 3039 E. London   Email: teach@quayeducation.co.uk
Tel: 020 8563 8885 W. London   Email: educate@quayeducation. co.uk
Tel: 0114 273 1616 Sheffield   Email: learn@quayeducation.co.uk
Fax: 0113 383 3745 Leeds   Email: develop@quayeducation.co.uk

Renaissance Education
Tel: 020 7712 1577
Email: teach@edulon.co.uk
South London

Select Education
Tel: 0845 600 1234
Email: education@selecteducation.com
Branches nationwide

Standby Teachers
Tel: 0800 146 471
Email: info@standbyteachers.com
Yorkshire

Termwise Teacher Recruitment
Tel: 01305 268 565
Email: info@termwise.co.uk
London and home counties

Teachers UK
Tel: 0800 068 1117
Email: education@teachers-uk.co.uk
London and home counties

Teaching Life 5
Tel: 0800 781 4572
Email: teachinglife5@aol.com
N.W. London, Luton, Herts, Birmingham, Cambridge

Timeplan
Tel: 0800 358 8040
Email: tes@timeplan.net
England and Scotland

Trust Education
Tel 020 7328 0000
Email: info@trusteducation.co.uk
London

Bibliography

Attwater, D. and John, C. (1982) *Dictionary of Saints*, London: Penguin.

Braithwaite, A. (2001) *When Uncle Bob Died*, Essex: Happy Cat Paperbacks.

Children's Britannica, London: Encyclopaedia Britannica International Ltd.

Kidwell, V. (2004) *Assemblies Made Easy*, London: Continuum International Publishing Group.

Levete, S. (1997) *When People Die*, London: Aladdin Books.

Mayo, S. and Jenkins, S. (1989) *On this day in History*, London: Armada Books.

Morris, L and Perkins, G. (1991) *Remembering Mum*, London: A & C Black.

Wimbs, D. (1999) *Freelance Copywriting*, London: A&C Black.

Suggested further reading

Bubb, S. (2003) *The Insiders' Guide for New Teachers*, London: Kogan and Page.

Bowden, D., Gray, B. and Thody, A. (2000) *The Teachers' Survival Guide, second edition*, London: Continuum International Publishing Group.

Cowley, S. (2003) *Guerilla Guide to Teaching*, London: Continuum International Publishing Group.

Cowley, S. (2002) *How to Survive your First Year in Teaching*, London: Continuum International Publishing Group.

Index

Whole chapters are in **bold**.